THE ARTIST AND HIS WORLD

General Editor of the Series: Jean Leymarie

Who was
Baudelaire ?

Critical Essay by

GEORGES POULET

Biographical Commentaries by

ROBERT KOPP

Translated by ROBERT ALLEN and JAMES EMMONS

The verse translations by Francis Duke on pages 24, 27, 38, 78, 79, 81, 82, 85-88
are reprinted by kind permission of the University of Virginia Press, Charlottesville, Virginia.

Plate on the title page:
Charles Meryon (1821-1868). The Morgue (detail), 1854. Etching.

Distributed in the United States by
THE WORLD PUBLISHING COMPANY
2231 West 110th Street, Cleveland, Ohio 44102

Library of Congress Catalog Card Number: 74-80456

CONTENTS

I

BIOGRAPHICAL COMMENTARIES BY ROBERT KOPP

II

CRITICAL ESSAY BY GEORGES POULET

*In the unsilvered mirror of time, we always recognize
Baudelaire, physically and morally, without ever having
seen him.*

Paul ELUARD

WHO was Baudelaire? The question is well worth asking. It is a simple one, and like all simple questions probably unanswerable. To whom, indeed, is one to turn for a reply? To the critics, of this century and last, who continually invent a Baudelaire of their own? To the poet himself, who all his life sounded the inner depths and tried to lay his heart bare? Should we turn to those who knew Baudelaire, who mixed with him and recorded their impressions of him? What a tissue of contradictions and misrepresentations in their accounts! All too often the man is identified with the work and credited with all the vices and failings so plainly displayed in that work. The judgment pronounced by a court of law against the *Flowers of Evil* in 1857 was actually no more than the official sanctioning of this "misunderstanding" of which Baudelaire, at the end of his life, thought of writing the history. But while one must be chary of identifying the man too closely with the work, it would be no less rash to separate the writer from his writings. To write is to body forth an inner world, and no French writer (except perhaps Balzac and Nerval) has lived his work with such intensity as Baudelaire; no writer's life has been to quite the same extent, not a work of art (that is rather the case of Chateaubriand), but an artistic creation. Asselineau, his first biographer, realized this: "Behind the written and published work there is a whole spoken, acted, experienced work which must be taken into account, because it explains the other and, as Baudelaire said himself, is the source from which the other sprang."

8

Paul Eluard

THE MIRROR OF BAUDELAIRE

It is obvious that Baudelaire was greatly served by his physique. How could such a man, made like none other to reflect doubt, hatred, contempt, disgust, melancholy, how could he display his passions so plainly and drain the world of its content in order to emphasize its disordered beauties, its sullied truths, sullied but so pliable and convenient? Why did he make it his business to carry on an uncompromising struggle against healthy reality, against that moral code fit for slaves which ensures the happiness and tranquillity of so-called free men? Why did he oppose evil in the making to ready-made good, the devil to God, intelligence to stupidity, clouds to clear and motionless skies? Hear him tell, and tell with desperate violence, what a liar he would be not to confess that the whole of himself is in his book. In spite of solitude, in spite of poverty, in spite of sickness, in spite of laws, he makes a clean breast of it, he keeps fighting. All the powers of misfortune are ranged on his side. Is there perhaps some chance of winning? Will black and white triumph over gray and dirt? Will the avenging hand finish writing, on the walls of the immense prison, the accursed phrase that will bring those walls crashing down? But the light is failing. The phrase was interminable. Baudelaire cannot see the words any more, the precious, mortal words. He is wounded by his own weapons. Once again he discovers his own end. Where the judges were powerless, sickness succeeds. Baudelaire is mute. On the other side of the walls, night begins to groan.

Alive yes, but *when he looked into the mirror he did not recognize himself and bowed*. So all is lost. Baudelaire, bowing to himself, thinks he is someone else. Definitely.

9

"*The poet*," he had written, "*enjoys this incomparable privilege, that he can be at once himself and someone else... For him alone, everything is vacant; and if certain places seem to be closed to him, it is simply that in his eyes they are not worth visiting.*" No place is visitable any more. Under stress of cold and hunger, of loneliness, of vain efforts to gain a hearing, of being the Enemy, he was carried off by weariness and death. Baudelaire yielded.

All that still remained were great fits of anger at the Nursing Sisters who attended him, who harshly (as his mother put it, though a very pious woman) tried to compel him to submit to their methods—anger remained, and swearing. When he left the St John and St Elizabeth Hospital, the Sisters called for purification ceremonies.

"*I can scarcely conceive (could my brain be a charmed mirror?) of any type of Beauty in which there is no Affliction.*" This responsiveness to Affliction makes Baudelaire an eminently modern poet, on the same grounds as Lautréamont and Rimbaud. At a time when the meaning of the word happiness is deteriorating day by day, until it has become a synonym of insensibility, this fatal responsiveness is the supernatural virtue of Baudelaire. This *charmed mirror* remains unclouded. Its purity prefers the darkness fraught with tears and dread, with dreams and stars, to the sorry processions of the midgets of the day, of the self-satisfied, their faces wreathed in complacent smiles. Everything reflected in that mirror gains by the strange light which all the shadows of a profoundly self-concerned life create and fortify, lovingly.

Though *guillotined*, he had a head of his own. None more lucid than he. No handsomer face than his. Matisse's portrait of him confirms what we had learned from Deroy, Courbet, Manet, Duchamp-Villon and all those wonderful photographs in which Baudelaire does not pose but outside place and space just goes on living, the apologist of dandyism, that is "*of all that smacks of opposition and revolt ... of all that is best in human pride.*" Nor has any man been so self-bedeviled.

Page 11: Baudelaire photographed by Nadar in 1862.

Page 12: Portrait of Baudelaire by Manet, 1865. Etching.

Page 13: Portrait of Baudelaire by Rouault, 1926. Lithograph.

Peint et Gravé par Manet. 1865   Imp. A. Salmon.

Baudelaire

14

While Rimbaud, since his death, has become the almost mythical figure celebrated in a recent book by Etiemble, Baudelaire became a legend in his lifetime. He got what he wanted (though he continually complained about it), for this pose was part of his system. The odd thing is that at first his legend reposed on silence: up to his thirtieth year Baudelaire gained his reputation as an unpublished author. He had published a few pages of art criticism, but no poetry, or very little, and that little under a borrowed name. Hence the wish expressed by Prarond, one of those who knew him best in the early days; much as he would have liked to, Prarond was unable to say much about his friend in the small ·volume of literary criticism, Some New Writers, which he published in 1852: "Among others, who we hope will not be lost from view, there is one poet above all who, in reciting occasionally for himself or for a few friends of poetry, has had the rare luck to acquire something almost like fame without publishing a line. This poet, who for an exhibition at the Louvre has written a whole catechism of modern painting, is Charles Baudelaire. Let him return to poetry and stick to it, and he will usefully occupy the first critic who attempts to carry on the work that I have here begun."

The legend of silence came to end with the publication of the eleven poems entitled Limbo in the Messager de l'Assemblée of April 9, 1851, a paper which had already published, the previous month, an initial version of Artificial Paradises, On Wine and Hashish.

Secretive and just a little eccentric before, now, in the Limbo poems, Baudelaire suddenly became alarming and almost monstrous. Henceforth the mystifier was caught in his own trap; he could never doff the mask and died the victim of the personage he had created. Convicted on false appearances, he tried in vain to prove his respectability by winning some official decoration or a seat at the French Academy. Before advising Baudelaire to withdraw, Sainte-Beuve had presented him in the following terms as a candidate for the seat at the Academy left vacant by the death of Lacordaire in 1861: "Where one had expected to see a strange, eccentric man appear, one finds oneself in the presence of a polite, respectful, exemplary candidate, a nice young man, of polished speech and well-bred in quite the classical manner."

LE TOMBEAU
DE CHARLES BAUDELAIRE

Le temple enseveli divulgue par la bouche
Sépulcrale d'égout bavant boue & rubis
Abominablement quelque idole Anubis
Tout le museau flambé comme un aboi farouche,

Ou que le gaz récent torde la mèche louche
Essuyeuse, on le sait, des opprobres subis,
Il allume hagard un immortel pubis
Dont le vol selon le réverbère découche.

Quel feuillage séché dans les cités sans soir
Votif pourra bénir comme elle se rasseoir
Contre le marbre vainement de Baudelaire

Au voile qui la ceint absente avec frissons
Celle son Ombre même un poison tutélaire
Toujours à respirer si nous en périssons.

137

Pages 14 and 15:
Portrait of Baudelaire by Matisse. Etching.
Illustration for "The Tomb of Charles Baudelaire" by Mallarmé.

Page 16:
Lycée Louis-le-Grand, Paris, in the time of Baudelaire.
Detail of a lithograph by Bachelier.

Childhood Regained

Genius is but *childhood regained* at will,
childhood endowed now with self-expression,
with mature organs and the analytical mind enabling
it to order the mass of materials
involuntarily accumulated.

Since Freud's findings gained currency, the part played by memories of early childhood and youth in the development of the individual has been generally recognized. While it is true that psychoanalysis continues to enhance our understanding of men and their works, we are too often inclined to forget the debt owed by psychoanalysis to the arts and in particular to literature. Here Baudelaire—like the Stendhal of the autobiographical writings—is in the position of a precursor. When, in *An Opium Eater*, he gives an account of the childhood impressions of Thomas De Quincey, whose work he assimilated, he first of all outlines, with the intuition of genius, the theory that was to be confirmed by lengthy scientific research half a century later. "It is in the observations on his childhood that we shall find the germ of the grown man's strange reveries and, in fine, of his genius. Every biographer has understood, to a greater or lesser extent, the importance of the anecdotes that cluster around the childhood of a writer or an artist. But I do not think that their importance has ever been strongly enough affirmed. Often, in contemplating works of art, not in their easily grasped *materiality*, in the over-clear hieroglyphics of their contours or in the obvious meaning of their subjects, but in the soul with which they are endowed, in the atmospheric impression they convey, in the spiritual light or darkness they shed upon our souls, I have felt myself possessed, as it were, by a vision of the childhood of their creators. Some small joy or sorrow of childhood, immeasurably magnified by an exquisite sensibility, later becomes, for the adult, the principle of a work of art, even though he may not be aware of it. To put it more briefly, would it not be possible to prove, by a philosophical comparison between the works of a mature artist and his state of mind as a child, that

genius is simply childhood clearly formulated, endowed, to express itself, with virile and potent means?"

In reading this passage, we cannot but regret more keenly that so little is known about Baudelaire's childhood and youth up to his return from his voyage to the South Seas. The letters from the schoolboy to his family, which were published in such unsatisfactory form a short time ago, contain nothing particularly new, and the best-documented episode of the period studied in this chapter is still the alleged voyage to India, on which Baudelaire himself never gave the slightest details, as though he desired to reserve his few exotic memories for his poetry alone. Thus, on the one hand, we have the voice of the young Baudelaire, but not—with a very few exceptions—those of the persons close to him; on the other, accounts by third parties, based on hearsay (except for that by Captain Saliz), or bare documents completely lacking in the warmth of life. This is certainly not very much.

Thus Baudelaire's youth can perforce be evoked only from the echoes of it he has left us and from our own intuition. The heredity we imagine is much more far-reaching in its effects than that objectively assigned to us by biology. And so Baudelaire could write: "My ancestors, idiots or maniacs, in the solemn gloom of their apartments, all victims of appalling passions."

His father was born in 1759. His mother, Caroline Dufays—the second wife of Joseph-François Baudelaire—in 1793. One during the Seven Years War, the other under the Terror (but in London). The first died in 1827, when the future poet was not yet six years old; the mother, however, outlived her son. From his first marriage, with Jeanne Janin, Joseph-François Baudelaire had an older son, Claude-

Alphonse. During the poet's adolescence, this half-brother, sixteen years his senior, tried to keep an eye on him, but finally became estranged from him.

"Let us reconstitute our memories," said Nerval. Baudelaire reconstituted his, summing up his childhood environment in these terms: "old Louis XVI furniture, antiques, Consulate, pastels, eighteenth-century society." A former student at the seminar of Sainte-Barbe—though there is no documentary evidence to show that he was ever ordained a priest, as his son asserted—Joseph-François Baudelaire became a tutor in the household of the Duc de Choiseul-Praslin shortly before the Revolution. He frequented Madame Helvetius's salon, where he became acquainted with the philosopher Condorcet and the physiologist Cabanis. Under the Empire, thanks to the good offices of the Duc de Choiseul, he was appointed "Secretary of the Administrative Commission and Controller of the Expenses of the Senate." In 1805 his situation improved when he became "Chief of the Offices of the Praetorship," in which capacity he was entitled to an apartment in the Luxembourg Gardens. An amateur painter, he won the friendship of Prud'hon and of such well-known artists of that day as the sculptor Claude Ramey and the painter Jean-Claude Naigeon. The inventory of his possessions after his death mentions, together with statuettes and drawings, some canvases by Greuze and a copy of Boilly's *Arrival of the Stagecoach.*

Thus, to his father, the poet may have owed—in addition to certain traits of character that were to be a burden to him, notably his physical weakness and instability—his initiation into the art of the last phase of the old regime and that "constant predilection, from childhood on, for painting and sculpture of every kind" which he repeatedly avowed.

Baudelaire's mother, Madame Aupick (as she became after her second marriage), remains something of a mystery. What was she really like? No record of her appearance survives. Of the arts, of literature, of poetry, she had not the slightest appreciation. She was conditioned to think, in discreet, guarded terms, of nothing but careers and worldly success. What could she understand of the disturbed, passionate youth of her son, except the need for achievement? "When I was a child," Baudelaire wrote to her on May 6, 1861, "I went through a period of passionate love for you; listen to me, don't be afraid to read on. I have never been so frank with you before. I remember a drive in a cab; you were leaving a nursing home to which you had been banished and, to prove that you had been thinking of your son, you showed me some pen-and-ink drawings you had done for me. Do you think I have a terrible memory? Later on... long walks, endless caresses... I existed only in you, and you belonged to me alone. You were at once my idol and my friend."

In his poems Baudelaire avoids any overly direct allusions to his private life, thus protecting himself against those commentators whose principal aim was to try to reach the man through the work. To this rule, there were two notable exceptions, to which Madame Aupick does not seem to have been particularly responsive, since her son wrote to her as follows on January 11, 1858: "You have apparently not noticed that the *Flowers of Evil* contains two poems about you, or at least alluding to intimate details of our past life, to the period of your widowhood which left me with such strange, unhappy memories... I have left these poems untitled and without any direct clues, as I cannot bring myself to profane the intimacies of family life."

Joseph-François Baudelaire was an amateur painter without much talent, as can be seen from a gouache of his that has been rediscovered: Love's Surprise, a frigid, painstaking allegory in the taste of the period. Despite his filial piety, Baudelaire was quite dispassionate in judging his father's painting. Thus, on December 30, 1857, he wrote to his mother: "A few months ago, in a dealer's in the Passage des Panoramas, I came across a painting by my father (a nude figure, a recumbent woman, seeing two other nude figures in a dream). I had no money at all, not even enough to put down a deposit, and since then the unbearable flood of daily futilities has been such that I have not pursued the matter. Do you think that many blunders of this kind have been committed? My father was a detestable artist; but all these old things have a moral value."

Joseph-François Baudelaire (1759-1827).
Love's Surprise, 1795-1796. Gouache.
Librairie Giraud-Badin, Paris.

Pierre-Paul Prud'hon (1758-1823).
Psyche carried off by the Zephyrs, about 1808. Black chalk.
Louvre, Paris.

Louis-Léopold Boilly (1761-1845).
The Arrival of the Stagecoach, 1803.
Oil Painting. Louvre, Paris.

The contrast is total between Baudelaire's father, the literate, erratic dilettante, and his father-in-law James Aupick, the career soldier "buttoned up tight in his rectitude"—as Jacques Crépet described him—"with his sword-arm ever at the ready." Aupick was one of the "new men"; his date of birth is unknown, but probably coincided with that of the Revolution, most likely being in the year of the Bastille. He recovered his virginity with each new regime. He had but one idea in his head: to succeed. And he did succeed. Except with his stepson, who was nevertheless so like him in his taste for honors: the poet was a candidate for the French Academy and hankered after the Legion of Honor and a post as manager of a subsidized theater. The disgraces he drew upon himself and experienced so intensely—his reduction to the status of a minor by the appointment of a guardian (1844) and his condemnation by the court of summary jurisdiction (1857)—were not so much protests against the social order as inverse recognitions of its power. In fact, paradoxical as it may seem, Aupick and Baudelaire were quite capable of getting along together, and the relations between them were at first quite good. Following Sartre, far too much has been made of Jules Buisson's tardily written and rather malicious testimony: "Baudelaire's mind was extremely delicate, refined, and original, but feminine and weak, and it cracked at the first shock. There was one event in his life that he was unable to bear: his mother's second marriage. On this subject he was inexhaustible and the wound bled ever afresh. There was no doubt about it, and his merciless logic on the subject could be summed up as follows: 'When you have a son like me'—'like me,' of course, being tacitly understood—'you do not remarry.'" Yet, in the letters addressed by Charles to his stepfather, there is no sign of animosity; Aupick is referred to as a "friend," even a "bosom friend."

Much later, Baudelaire confessed to his mother: "You know what a frightful education your husband tried to give me; I am forty years old and still cannot think without pain of school or of the fear my stepfather inspired in me. Yet I loved him, and I have by now acquired sufficient wisdom to do him justice."

Baudelaire as a Schoolboy, 1833-1834. Photograph
of a Miniature. Armand Godoy Collection, Lausanne.

*In 1832 Colonel Aupick was transferred to Lyons. Charles,
then aged eleven, had to bid farewell to the parks, toyshops,
and sweetshops of Paris and was swallowed up in the fog
of Lyons, which he would always recall with horror. After
spending a few months at the Pension Delorme—"dirty,
ill-kept, untidy"—he entered the Collège Royal, where at
least he appreciated the food. His family lived in the Rue
d'Auvergne, "one of the finest in Lyons"; the wood engraving
by Fonville shows the splendid view that extended from it
beyond the Rhone to the "rich" and "green" hillside of
Fourvière. When Aupick returned to Paris in 1836, it was
to present the headmaster of the Collège Louis-le-Grand with
a choice student, a prizeman in the Concours général.
In April 1839, however, he was dismissed by the headmaster
for some trifling misdemeanor, "despite his quite remarkable
capacities," because of the "very bad spirit from which the
good order of the college has more than once had to suffer."*

Anonymous Portrait of General Aupick on Horseback, 1841.
Pencil. Mrs Ronald Davis Collection, Paris.

Page 23:
View of Lyons in 1851. Woodcut by Fonville.

He studied privately and in August 1839 he passed his Baccalaureate examination safely, but without any great distinction. By enrolling for courses at the School of Law in 1839-1840, he was able to keep up the polite fiction of responsibility cherished by his family circle.

The reality was, however, very different. "A free existence in Paris, first literary connections: Ourliac, Nerval, Balzac, Le Vavasseur, De Latouche," Baudelaire noted. It is probable that he exaggerated the extent of his acquaintanceship, for he had no ties with either Nerval or Henri De Latouche.

Balzac he met from time to time after getting to know him quite by chance. He told Prarond about it the day after their first meeting: "Balzac and Baudelaire were walking along in opposite directions beside the Seine (on the left bank).

Baudelaire stopped in front of Balzac and began to laugh as if he had known him for ten years. Balzac, too, stopped, and replied with a great guffaw as though he had just encountered a long-lost friend. And these two kindred spirits, after recognizing one another at a glance and exchanging greetings, walked on together, absorbed in conversation and argument, neither being in the least surprised by the other." But this account, too, may be quite fictitious. There could hardly have been much fellow-feeling between two such dissimilar temperaments, and Baudelaire, a few years later, in his essay How to Pay Your Debts When You Are a Genius (1845), related with biting severity one of those indiscretions of which Balzac was sometimes guilty without even being aware of it.

Place de l'Estrapade, Paris, in 1839.
Lithograph by Champin from a drawing by Régnier.

The place where he met his friends during this period was the Pension Bailly et Levêque, 11 place de l'Estrapade, a sort of forerunner of today's cultural centers for young people, whose owner, a printer by trade, provided students with libraries and meeting-rooms opening on a large garden and organized lectures there. However, according to the lodgers Baudelaire met there, life in this Pension was lighthearted and dissipated rather than studious, and his less reputable acquaintances included Sarah, a small-time Latin Quarter prostitute, of whom he had far from happy memories:

Your bed might entertain the universe,
Wanton, whom boredom makes the more perverse!
To fit your teeth for that peculiar play,
Your trough must offer one fresh heart each day.

There was no disputing the evidence. Charles kept low company. He prided himself particularly on his freedom from conventional moral restraints and, in 1839, confessed to his brother that he had contracted a venereal infection. The family felt threatened in itself and in its hopes. So

Charles had to be sent on a long voyage to change his outlook and to remove him from his dangerous environment: "to shake off," his brother Alphonse wrote to him, "the filth that surrounds you."

Aupick (who by now was a general) held options even on the sea, by the shores of which he had grown up, at Gravelines. He arranged to have Baudelaire entrusted to Captain Saliz, who was sailing to Calcutta on the Paquebot-des-Mers-du-Sud; but Baudelaire parted company with him after a rough crossing. "Voyages to India: first adventure, ship loses mast: Mauritius, Bourbon Island, Malabar, Ceylon, Hindustan, the Cape; pleasant outings. Second adventure: return journey on a foundering ship with no food supplies." This extract from the autobiographical note written by Baudelaire for Duranty, round about 1861, is misleading in a way that has had far-reaching consequences. Generation after generation has believed in Baudelaire's famous voyage to India. In reality, he did not get any farther than the Mascarene islands in the Indian Ocean. There, on Mauritius, he was given a friendly welcome by a French colonial family, the Autard de Bragards. The mistress of the household, whose brother had an estate in the Pamplemousses district, where Bernardin de Saint-Pierre had situated the action of Paul and Virginia, *expressed the desire to read something by Baudelaire. He sent the poem that was to be entitled* To a Creole Lady *in the* Flowers of Evil, *not directly to the subject of his inspiration but, out of courtesy, to her husband, in a letter dated October 20, 1841: "As it is good, right, and proper that lines addressed to a lady by a young man should pass through her husband's hands before reaching her, I am sending them to you, so that you need show them to her only if you would like to do so." This was certainly rather an odd procedure for the budding dandy. Baudelaire was aware of this, for he wrote in the same letter: "If I did not love Paris and miss it so much, I should stay as long as possible with you and force you to like me and find me a little less 'baroque' than I seem."* To a Creole Lady *was the first poem to be published under Baudelaire's signature and appeared in* L'Artiste *in 1845. While traveling back to France, Madame Autard de Bragard died at sea, at the age of thirty-nine, on June 22, 1857, in the very week that saw the publication of the* Flowers of Evil.

Port Louis on the Island of Mauritius, 1850. Drawing and lithograph by L. Le Breton.

Anonymous Portrait of Madame Autard de Bragard, about 1840. Oil painting. Collection of Baronne La Caze, Paris.

TO A CREOLE LADY

In perfumed lands that genial suns caress,
I met, beneath a purple canopy
Of palms that drench the eyes with drowsiness,
A modest creole lady of quality.

A warmly pallid brunette sorceress
Who bends her head in graceful dignity,
A huntress by her height and slenderness,
Her tranquil smile, her calm confiding eye.

In glory's land, Madame, if you should reign
Along the verdant strand of Loire or Seine,
An ornament to any noble seat,

You'd sow the seeds of sonnets to be made
Among the poets lingering in the shade,
And make their willing slavery complete.

English translation by Francis Duke
reprinted by courtesy of the
University of Virginia Press

Page 28: Letter from Baudelaire to Sainte-Beuve, about 1843. Spoelberch de Lovenjoul Library, Chantilly, near Paris.

Monsieur,

Stendhal a dit quelque part —
Ceci ou à peu près — : J'écris pour
une dizaine d'âmes que je ne verrai
peut-être jamais, mais que j'adore
pour les avoir vues.

Ces paroles, Monsieur, ne sont elles
pas une excellente excuse pour les
importuns, et n'est il pas clair que
tout écrivain est responsable des
sympathies qu'il éveille?

Ces vers ont été faits pour vous —
Et si naïvement — que lorsqu'ils
furent achevés, je me suis demandé
s'ils ne ressemblaient pas à une
impertinence, — et si la personne
louée — n'avait pas le droit de
s'offenser de l'éloge — j'attends que
vous daigniez m'en dire votre avis

Dandy, Poet, Art Critic

Romantic art means modern art,
and that means inwardness,
spirituality, color, aspiration toward the infinite,
expressed by all the resources art has to offer.

BAUDELAIRE returned from Mauritius on the *Alcide* which, after calling at the Cape, dropped anchor in Bordeaux harbor on February 16, 1842. He wrote at once to his stepfather: "Here I am back from my long trip. I got in yesterday evening, having left Bourbon on November 4. I haven't brought back a penny *and I have often lacked the bare necessaries...* I think I have come back a wiser man." All this was not very reassuring and the last statement was belied by the haughty, offhand tone of the letter. His family awaited him with a certain anxiety, half expecting the worst. Even before he had seen his half-brother again, Claude-Alphonse Baudelaire wrote to General Aupick: "Let us try to welcome Charles today like the prodigal son coming home: either he has recognized the error of his ways and the fear of confessing it holds him back and prevents him from writing, or he has not changed." Already plans were being laid to tame the rebel, whose mind was set on art and literature, and make him settle down to bourgeois respectability. A tour of duty in the army, it was thought, might do the trick, unless he was lucky enough to escape conscription or purchase a substitute. To prevent that, the money he stood to inherit must be kept out of his hands. Lawyer Ancelle, a friend of the family, would see to that.

As it turned out, all these calculations went wrong. He was not called up, and when he came of age, on April 9, 1842, he entered into possession of a small fortune, some 70,000 francs (about 14,000 dollars). This capital he broke into at once. In June he took an apartment in the Ile Saint-Louis, where he lived for the next three years. At that time it was an odd place to choose, already indicative of Baudelaire's originality and dandyish eccentricity. His friends were surprised. Prarond wrote: "The Ile Saint-Louis

seemed to us remoter than Mauritius. 'You will pine away out there,' I told him. 'No,' he said, 'the fox loves his burrow.'" It was a solitary, mysterious part of Paris, difficult of access, and one had to pay, for there was a toll bridge. It was inhabited chiefly by artisans, *rentiers*, and artists, who were attracted by the low rents. The painter Meissonier lived there before Baudelaire; it was not until after he left that Daumier took a studio in the Ile.

There, first on the Quai de Béthune, then in the historic town house called the Hôtel Pimodan, Baudelaire led the carefree life of a rich dandy with expensive tastes. He became known as one of the best dressed men in Paris, in his dark swallow-tail coat, white shirt of the finest linen with a turn-down collar and a cravat of oxblood red, top hat, and light pink gloves. Thus he is described by Nadar, Asselineau, and Gautier. Le Vavasseur likened him to "Byron tailored by Brummel." Keenly interested in the arts, Baudelaire did not feel it was enough to surround himself with fine old furniture; he had to have a collection of old master paintings. He found what he wanted in the back shop of a second-hand dealer who lived next door and supplied him at bargain prices with Tintorettos, Correggios, Poussins and a Velazquez or two—all copies, of course.

His family was alarmed at the rate of expenditure. Acting out of a quite understandable desire to preserve at least half the capital (by now the other half had been spent), his family arranged, on September 21, 1844, to have it administered by a guardian, Lawyer Ancelle. So legally Baudelaire reverted to the status of a minor, receiving an allowance from the lawyer. It was hardly enough for him to live on, and to the end of his life he was driven to various shifts or fell back on his mother's purse.

This situation was the more humiliating for him since he was determined to pursue an independent way of life, with no ties of any kind. "To make me swallow the pill," he wrote to his mother, "you keep telling me that there is nothing unnatural or dishonoring in all this. It may be so, and I'm willing to believe it. But what does it matter how it really is for most people, if for me it is *something quite different*... One thing you must get into your head, which you never seem to realize, and that is that unfortunately for me I am not made as other men are." For the rest of his life Baudelaire looked for salvation to the cancellation of this guardianship, which condemned him to "a double, contradictory life, honored on one side, odious and scorned on the other." For him it was a paralyzing contradiction, depriving him of the energy needed to organize a life which he felt was not entirely in his own hands, and for which he accordingly refused to assume full responsibility.

The discouragement born of this situation, which had been brought about by his own fault, led finally to a suicide attempt in June 1845. The attempt miscarried, perhaps he meant it to, for with a deep and genuine distaste for life there was mingled a sincere desire to win back the affection of his family, and no doubt to obtain payment of his debts. "I'm killing myself, without sorrow... I'm killing myself because I can't go on living, the weariness of going to sleep and the weariness of waking up are unbearable. I'm killing myself because I'm of no use to anyone, *and dangerous to myself*. I'm *killing* myself because I believe myself immortal, and *I hope*."

His belongings he bequeathed to Jeanne Duval, whom he had met shortly after his return from overseas; his manuscripts he left to the poet Théodore de Banville.

But he soon recovered, and went back to his parents for a time, who were living at 7 Place Vendôme; since November 1842 General Aupick, rising irresistibly in the scale of promotion, had been commanding officer of Paris and the Department of the Seine. But there was no peace in the family, new disagreements arose, and again Baudelaire broke away angrily.

By the fall of 1845 we find him living in a small hotel in Rue Laffitte, near the Opera. This was only the first of more than thirty temporary lodgings occupied by Baudelaire up to the end of his life. Dogged by creditors, he tried in vain for the space of twenty years to find a settled home where he could work in peace. Periodically he kept a woman with him, for he needed *"a family at all costs,"* as he wrote to his mother on December 4, 1854. Again and again he tried to settle down with a mulatto girl or quadroon named Jeanne, of whom very little is known; it is not even certain whether her surname was Duval, Lemer or Prosper.

There are conflicting accounts of Jeanne; some describe her as stupid, ugly and shrewish, others as an authentic tropical beauty. What is quite certain is that Baudelaire was profoundly attached to her; she inspired some of his finest poems, *Exotic Perfume, Hair, Sed non satiata, The Balcony, A Ghost*. Toward her, his feelings were at first those of a lover, then of a brother, finally of a father. But it was a stormy relationship. He broke with her many times. On one such occasion he wrote to his mother (September 11, 1856): "I know in my heart that whatever agreeable adventure may come my way, pleasure, money, or vanity, I shall always regret that woman who was my only distraction, my only pleasure, my only comrade."

"Amatory Mysteries
of the Theaters of Paris."
Vignette by Nadar.
Cazel Publisher, Paris 1844.

Page 32:
Emile Deroy (1820-1846).
Portrait of Baudelaire
(detail), 1843 or 1844.
Oil painting.
Musée National, Versailles.

On his return from overseas, Baudelaire fell in again with his friends from the Pension Bailly: Ernest Prarond, Gustave Le Vavasseur, Philippe de Chennevières, Auguste Dozon, Jules Buisson. They had been brought together by a common taste for literature, and some of them, like Prarond and Le Vavasseur, were already budding poets. They proposed to Baudelaire to publish a book of their poems together, sharing expenses; at Baudelaire's suggestion, Dozon joined them. "Baudelaire," wrote Le Vavasseur, "had given me his manuscripts. They contained in rough outline some of the pieces since published in the Flowers of Evil *(Spleen and Ideal). Without beating about the bush I made some comments on them, and rash and indiscreet friend that I was, I even wanted to* correct *the poet. Baudelaire said nothing, kept his temper perfectly and withdrew his poems from the book. Very wise of him: his material was of an altogether different make from our rough cloth, and we appeared alone." And so the slender volume of* Verses *was published in 1843 under the names of Le Vavasseur, Prarond and Argonne (the pseudonym of Dozon); but there is reason to think that some of the pieces published over Prarond's signature were actually written by Baudelaire.*

About the same period Baudelaire had a share in a projected verse drama called Ideolus; *the manuscript has survived and most of it is in Prarond's hand. It was about 1843 too that he sent to Sainte-Beuve—one of the writers most admired by Baudelaire and his friends—a letter accompanied by a poem in which Baudelaire expressed, in chiseled lines which are difficult to translate, the impact made on him by Sainte-Beuve's novel* Volupté:

I've dipped at large into the mystery deep
Of this your book so dear to torpid souls
Whom fate has afflicted with like complaints...

According to Prarond, many of the poems published years later in the Flowers of Evil *had already been written, or at least sketched out, for Baudelaire was a careful and exacting workman and revised them all many times.*
At that time his work as a poet, though quietly and steadily pursued in private, was overshadowed by his activity as a journalist and art critic. Baudelaire made his début as a writer and reviewer for some of the smaller Paris papers. He became a regular contributor to the Corsaire-Satan *in which he published reviews and humorous essays like* How to Pay Your Debts When You are a Genius, *a* Choice of Consoling Maxims on Love, *and the* Advice to Young Writers. *When he sent a copy of his* Consoling Maxims *to his sister-in-law, Madame Claude-Alphonse Baudelaire, he announced his intention of writing a* Catechism of the Woman Woo'd: "I want the lover who really loves to be constant, and here is just one article of my catechism to show you what I mean: Love well, vigorously, gallantly, orientally, fiercely the woman you woo, let not your love torment another's love." In these early writings one glimpses an optimistic, high-spirited Baudelaire, quite different from the usual image of a sardonic, ill-fated poet. The young writer had no hesitation about contributing unsigned pieces to satirical miscellanies like the* Salon caricatural *and* Causeries du Tintamarre, *even to a libellous volume called* Mystères galans des théâtres de Paris. *The best picture we have of the young Baudelaire was sketched out by Baudelaire himself in* La Fanfarlo, *published in 1847, the only story he ever wrote: it marks the end of his literary apprenticeship.*

Page 35:
Caricature of Baudelaire by Nadar, 1854.
Charcoal and gouache.
Bibliothèque Nationale, Paris.

Félix Nadar in 1860 at the age of forty,
photographed by his brother Adrien Tournachon.

While in his twenties Baudelaire contributed not only to the smaller papers but also to several anonymous volumes of satire, such as the Salon caricatural *(1846)* and the Mystères galans *(1844)*. These "Mysteries," reprinted in 1938 by Jacques Crépet, are in fact a miscellany of short stories and show world gossip. Among the contributors were several well-known figures in the Bohemian world of Paris: Mathieu-Dairnvaell, Fortuné Mesuré, Abbé Constant, Privat d'Anglemont. Baudelaire's main contribution was an amusing squib against François Ponsard, a popular dramatist. The book was published by "Cazel," a cover name for the bookseller Le Gallois. The mask with gaping jaws on the jacket was drawn by Nadar. The little scene at the top was a dig aimed by the publisher at the actress Rachel in particular, who had sued him when, a short time before, he had advertised a forthcoming book entitled Les Actrices galantes ("Amorous Actresses"). The book had to be withdrawn and Le Gallois had to publish an apology. What he had done now was simply to bring out the book under another title and under an assumed name, "Cazel"; and deaf to his victims' protests he redoubled his attacks: the figure at the top holds a banner reading: "very amorous actresses." The horned ogre, its teeth inscribed NOUS VERON (a pun on the phrase "We shall see"), is a caricature of the well-known Dr. Véron, former director of the Opera and publisher of the magazine Revue de Paris, a man much feared in the theatrical world, as he could make or break a reputation.

Nadar met Baudelaire in 1843 or 1844 and became one of his closest friends; he is the only person whom Baudelaire in his letters addresses as "tu" instead of "vous." Extraordinarily versatile, a writer, a caricaturist, an outstanding photographer, an aeronaut (from whom Jules Verne got ideas for his early science-fiction novels), he wrote one of the best accounts of the poet, Charles Baudelaire intime. Baudelaire described him as "a man of the most astonishing vitality," adding: "It has made me envious to see how well he succeeds in everything that is not abstract." Among Nadar's many caricatures of Baudelaire, made at intervals from 1852 to 1859, the one reproduced here is perhaps the most expressive. At the top, written in Nadar's hand, is a remark dropped by Baudelaire: "Every revolution has as its corollary the massacre of the innocents."

BEGINNER'S LUCK
AND BAD LUCK

by Baudelaire

Young writers who in speaking of another young writer say in an envious tone of voice, "It's a good start, he's had a stroke of luck!" fail to consider that every start has its antecedents; it is the outcome of twenty false starts of which they know nothing.

I question whether a writer's reputation has ever been made overnight. I rather think his success comes, in arithmetical or geometric proportions according to his powers, as a result of previous successes, often invisible to the naked eye. There is a slow accumulation of molecular successes; never any such thing as sudden and miraculous flowerings.

Those who say, "I'm unlucky," are those who have not yet had enough successes and are unaware of the fact.

I make allowance for the thousand circumstances by which the human will is hemmed in and which have their legitimate causes. They are a circumference enclosing the will. But that circumference is a shifting, turning, living thing, its circle and center change every day, every minute, every second. Thus, swept along by it, all the human wills which it shuts in vary their reciprocal workings at every moment, and this is what constitutes liberty.

Liberty and fatality are two contraries; seen at close range and at a distance, they are a single will.

That is why there is no such thing as bad luck. If you are unlucky, then you lack something. Find out what that something is, and study the working of nearly related wills so that you may more easily shift the circumference.

La Fanfarlo —

La Fanfarlo. Pencil drawing by Baudelaire.
Armand Godoy Collection, Lausanne.

Jeanne Duval, 1858-1860. Pen drawing by Baudelaire.
Armand Godoy Collection, Lausanne.

Page 37: Jeanne Duval, 1865. Pen drawing by Baudelaire.
Armand Godoy Collection, Lausanne.

Dessin de
Baudelaire.
27. fév.
1865

quærens
quem
devoret.

37

THE BALCONY

Unrivalled mistress, memory's potent drug,
You who are all my pleasure, all my duty,
Those fireside evenings, magic, warm, and snug,
You must recall, and our caresses' beauty,
Unrivalled mistress, memory's potent drug!

Beside the hearth aglow with throbbing coals,
Or on the balcony in rosy mist,
What deathless vows, exchanged by throbbing souls!
How sweet your breast and heart seemed as we kissed
Beside the hearth aglow with throbbing coals!

How fair the sun of those warm evening skies!
How bold the heart! How vast infinity!
As I bent down, my queen to idolize,
I thought I breathed her blood's suave fragrancy!
How fair the sun of those warm evening skies!

The night drew closer like a panelled wall,
As my eyes, seeking yours, the darkness scanned.
I drank your breath, that nectar and that gall!
Your foot lay safe in my fraternal hand,
And night drew closer like a panelled wall.

My happiest memories I recall to mind
When on your knees I live again my past,
For where should I such soft enchantments find
But in your body and your heart amassed,
My happiest memories to recall to mind?

Will vows, scents, kisses in infinitude
Arise to life again from gulfs unsounded
As the suns rise again, their youth renewed,
Fresh from their baths in ocean depths unbounded?
Ah, vows, scents, kisses in infinitude!

English translation by Francis Duke
reprinted by courtesy of the
University of Virginia Press

Edouard Manet (1832-1883). Baudelaire's Mistress, 1862. Oil painting. Museum of Fine Arts, Budapest.

Eugène Delacroix (1798-1863).
Women of Algiers in their Apartment,
1834. Oil painting. Louvre, Paris.

◄ Eugène Delacroix (1798-1863).
Hamlet bent on Following his
Father's Ghost, 1835. Lithographic stone.
Delacroix Museum, Paris.

"Along with the gift of poetry, Baudelaire had very early a passion for all the arts," wrote Prarond. In the years 1842-1846 "he was as much concerned with painting as with poetry." Prarond adds: "I sometimes went with him to the Louvre, which he rarely passed without entering. He especially liked to linger in the gallery of Spanish masters, then much richer than it is now in ferocious paintings; most of these torture pictures were owned by King Louis-Philippe and he took them back in 1848. Baudelaire had his infatuations and was much struck by an El Greco; he would go in to look at two or three pictures and then be off. He was beginning to talk about the moderns. I need hardly say how much he admired Delacroix. Among the draftsmen, as he sometimes had strong likes and dislikes, he revered Daumier and detested Gavarni."

Baudelaire gained a reputation as an art critic before he was known at all as a poet. Although he later disowned his Salon of 1845, *his insight is already plain in those pages. He paid tribute to Delacroix as the "most original painter of past and modern times." He especially admired the* Sultan of Morocco with his Bodyguard and Officers, *a picture "so harmonious, in spite of the splendor of the tones, that it is gray, gray as nature, gray as the summer atmosphere when the sun seems to throw a haze of trembling dust over each object... The composition has something unexpected about it because it is true and natural." After the marvelous pictures of Delacroix, the "outstanding piece of the exhibition" was William Haussoullier's* Fountain of Youth *(which has recently come to light in an English collection). It was not only to defend this young, unknown painter against the*

Eugène Delacroix (1798-1863).
The Sultan of Morocco receiving the
French Ambassador, Count de Mornay, 1832.
Oil sketch for the painting exhibited at the 1845 Salon.
P. Grandville Collection, Paris.

sarcasm of the public that Baudelaire praised this rather naïve composition in the "troubadour" style, a style which originated in the eighteenth century and reached the height of its popularity after the Restoration of 1815. Unlike his fellow critics, who were put off by the artist's high-pitched colors, Baudelaire complimented Haussoullier on his "very showy" painting: "The color is terrible, inexorable in its shrillness, and would be overbold if the artist were less sturdy a man; but as it is the color has distinction, a merit so much sought after by the gentlemen of the school of Ingres." The fact that Baudelaire took care to qualify his praise shows that, in spite of his enthusiasm for an unusual picture, he saw the dangers of an academicism carried to the point of pastiche.

Although Baudelaire had no special fondness for landscape painting, he spoke discerningly in his first Salons of Théodore Rousseau and Corot, both of whom were still considered minor artists. Corot "paints like the great masters," "he knows how to be a colorist within a narrow range of tones" and "he is always a harmonist even with fairly raw, fairly bright colors. His composition is always impeccable. Thus in Homer and the Shepherds there is nothing unnecessary, nothing to pare away, not even the two little figures together as they go down the path."

In the sculpture section Baudelaire acknowledged the superior skill of the French artists but thought them too much concerned with technique and preferred the exhibit submitted by the Florentine sculptor Bartolini, an early friend of

William Haussoullier (1818-1891).
The Fountain of Youth, 1843.
Oil painting.
Graham Reynolds Collection, London.

Camille Corot (1796-1875).
Homer and the Shepherds, 1845.
Oil painting.
Musée Municipal, Saint-Lô.

Ingres. He was one of the few critics to single out Bartolini's Nymph with a Scorpion, *which he admired for its "taste, nobility, grace" and "chastity of line which by no means excludes originality."*
Baudelaire's Salon of 1845, *a slender volume of art criticism still traditional-minded but full of bold insights, ends with an appeal in favor of the art of the future, or rather of the* present. *"No one is listening to see how the wind will blow tomorrow ; and yet the heroism of* modern life *surrounds and presses upon us... The* painter, *the true painter, will be he who can extract from present-day life its epic quality, and make us see and understand, through color and line, how great and poetic we are in our cravats and patent-leather boots."*

The Ingres Room at the Bonne-Nouvelle Bazaar Exhibition. Print from "L'Illustration," February 14, 1846.

It has long been a stereotype of art criticism to oppose Delacroix the colorist to Ingres the draftsman, and it is assumed that Baudelaire, as the ardent defender of Delacroix, must have despised Ingres. This is a mistake. The poet-critic was never the exclusive admirer of a single school. Though for some years Ingres had ceased to exhibit at the annual Salons, Baudelaire in his Salon of 1845 *made a point of paying tribute to him, and this in connection with Delacroix: "We know of only two men in Paris who draw as well as Delacroix, one in a similar way, the other by a contrary method. One is Daumier, the caricaturist; the other is Ingres, the great painter, the artful worshipper of Raphael. This may amaze both their friends and enemies, their followers and antagonists; but a slow and considered scrutiny will show that these three different kinds of drawing have this in common, that they perfectly and completely render the side of nature they mean to render, and that they say just what they mean to say."*

A few months later, in reviewing the benefit exhibition organized by the Society of Artists in the galleries of the Bonne-Nouvelle Bazaar, near the Porte Saint-Denis, Baudelaire again seized the opportunity to emphasize the variety of his tastes. A special room was set aside for eleven pictures by Ingres, representing each period of his career. "Our annual Salon exhibitions, turbulent, noisy and overcrowded, can give no idea of this one, which is as staid and serious as a scholar's study... The classical exhibition was greeted at first by a loud burst of laughter from our younger artists. Most of these presumptuous gentlemen... are incapable of understanding these austere lessons in revolutionary painting, painting that voluntarily dispenses with meretricious charms and appeals above all to the mind and soul, painting bitter and despotic as the revolution from which it sprang." In the Ingres room were the Stratonice, *"which would have astonished Poussin," the portraits of Bertin, Molé and Madame d'Haussonville, "true portraits, by which I mean the ideal reconstruction of individuals," and several* Odalisques, *on which Baudelaire commented as follows: "One thing, as we see it, that chiefly distinguishes Ingres' talent is his love of women. His libertinism is serious and full of conviction. Ingres is never so happy or so powerful as when his genius comes to grips with the charms of a young beauty. The muscles, the folds of the flesh, the shadowed dimples, the hilly undulations of the skin, nothing is overlooked. If the isle of Cythera were to order a picture from Ingres, you may be quite sure it would not be blithe and smiling like Watteau's, but robust and satisfying like antique love."*

The second attraction of this show were ten canvases by David, including The Death of Socrates, Telemachus and Eucharis, Bonaparte at the Mont Saint-Bernard *("with Gros's picture of him in the* Battle of Eylau, *the only poetic and grandiose Bonaparte that France possesses") and above all* Marat. *"The divine* Marat, *with one arm hanging out of the tub and limply holding its last pen, his chest pierced with the sacrilegious wound, has just breathed his last. On a green writing stand in front of him his hand still holds the treacherous letter. 'Citizen, that I should be so miserable gives me sufficient claim on your benevolence.' The bath water is red with blood, the paper is blood-stained; on the floor lies a large kitchen knife soaked in blood; on*

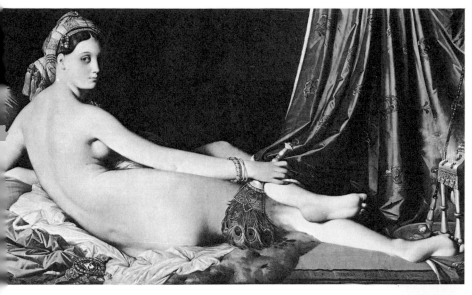

Jean-Dominique Ingres (1780-1867).
The Large Odalisque, 1814.
Oil painting.
Louvre, Paris.

Jacques-Louis David (1748-1825).
The Death of Marat, 1793.
Oil painting.
Musées Royaux des Beaux-Arts,
Brussels.

a wretched packing case which made up the tireless journal-
ist's working furniture, we read: 'To Marat, David.' All
these details are as real and historical as a Balzac novel.
The drama is there, alive in all its sickening horror, and by
a strange tour de force *which makes this picture David's*
masterpiece and one of the great wonders of modern art,
there is nothing trivial or ignoble about it."
But Baudelaire did not stop there. He went on to praise
Guérin and Girodet, "steadfast and invulnerable fragments
of that great school" of David, as well as Prud'hon, "brother
in Romanticism to André Chénier," whose "soft, invisible,
stealthy line, winding beneath the color, is a legitimate sub-
ject for surprise, especially when you consider the period."
Gros and Géricault he described as "generous temperaments."
Only Baron Gérard, "eager to please everyone," was re-
proached for his "courtier-like eclecticism."

Eugène Delacroix (1798-1863). Pietà for the Church of Saint-Denis du Saint-Sacrement, 1843. Oil sketch. Louvre, Paris.

The Salon of 1846, both in form and matter, was very different from that of the year before. In 1845 Baudelaire had kept to the method of his predecessors, dealing successively with the different types of work: history paintings, portraits, genre pictures, landscapes, drawings and engravings, sculptures. Each of these headings is followed by a critical listing of artists and works with Baudelaire's comments on them. In spite of the originality of his comments, it was a quite conventional presentation, simply following the order of the exhibition itself.

It was no doubt for this reason, and lest it be noticed how much he owed in the way of ideas and phrasing to the art writings of Diderot, Heine and Stendhal (borrowings which, however, in the Salon of 1846 were much more numerous and indeed were carried at times to the point of plagiarism), that Baudelaire later refused to allow the Salon of 1845 to be included in the collected edition of his works. According to Champfleury and Monselet, he went so far as to burn the remaining copies of his first Salon review, which had been published in the form of a booklet.

In the Salon of 1846, on the other hand, he took the opportunity afforded by a review of the exhibition to set down his ideas on the purpose of art criticism and the state of contemporary art. This he does methodically in eighteen carefully planned chapters in which theoretical and thematic remarks alternate with analysis and description. His comments on the works exhibited are usually brief and always lead to considerations of a general nature, for "criticism touches at every moment on metaphysics."

It is probable that for this study of contemporary painting, prompted by the annual Salon exhibition, Baudelaire was drawing on notes compiled earlier for another book which was never published, though the year before on the cover of the Salon of 1845 it had been announced as "forthcoming": an essay entitled On Modern Painting.

No one questioned Baudelaire's natural eye for painting, and in 1845, rather than judging pictures by well-defined aesthetic standards, he simply invented reasons to justify his likes and dislikes. In the Salon of 1846 his approach was quite different: "I sincerely believe that the best criticism is one that is amusing and poetic; not a cold, algebraic criticism which, under the pretext of explaining everything, has neither love nor hate and deliberately strips itself of every shred of temperament. No, the best criticism, since a fine picture is nature reflected by an artist, will be that picture reflected by an intelligent and sensitive mind. Thus the best account of a picture may well be a sonnet or an elegy. But this kind of criticism is destined for books of poems and readers of poetry. As for criticism properly so called, I hope the philosophers will grasp what I am going to say: to be just, that is to justify its existence, criticism should be partial, passionate and political, in other words written from an exclusive point of view, but from the point of view that opens up the widest horizons."

It would be a mistake however, he then goes on to say, to judge a work of art on the basis of some general rule, extolling line for example to the detriment of color or vice versa. The ideal point of view cannot be preselected by the art critic, it is imposed on him by the work he is dealing with. The critic's task is first to understand what the artist was about, what his intention was, and then to gauge the extent to which he achieved it.

The first quality required of an artist is "naivety and the sincere expression of his temperament furthered by every means which his technique provides." For "an artist without temperament is not worthy to paint pictures."

The best works, moreover, are also those which are produced from a distinct and exclusive point of view, from that of color (Delacroix) or that of line (Ingres), and art's worst enemies are the "imitators" and the "eclectics" (Horace Vernet, Ary Scheffer), all those painters who depend for their effects on the application of ready-made formulas. From now on Baudelaire's sound judgment enabled him to be as firm in disparagement as in praise.

But his desire to appreciate fairly the originality and value of each of the works deriving from different trends did not exclude a marked preference for the colorists. Color in Baudelaire's eyes meant Romanticism, in other words modernity, for "Romanticism is the most recent, the most topical expression of the beautiful." Color is "idealistic," "spiritualistic," it makes one "dream and glimpse beyond," while line is "materialistic" and "naturalistic." For Baudelaire the crux of the matter lay in overcoming the antagonism between "supernaturalism" and "modernity."

Eugène Delacroix (1798-1863). The Death of Sardanapalus, 1826. Oil sketch. Louvre, Paris.

◄ Eugène Delacroix (1798-1863). The Abduction of Rebecca, 1846. Oil painting. The Metropolitan Museum of Art, New York. Wolfe Fund, 1903.

Romanticism and color led Baudelaire straight to Eugène Delacroix, the foremost romantic painter of the day, whom the "majority of the public" had "a long time ago, indeed from his very first work, placed at the head of the modern school." This statement, in its bold emphasis, comes rather as a surprise; it is a further indication of the distance separating the Salon of 1846 from that of 1845. Though he had nothing but praise for Delacroix in 1845, he does not seem to have recognized him as the painter of modern life, since for Baudelaire, as a convinced disciple of Stendhal and Balzac, to paint modern life meant representing people in contemporary dress. The 1845 Salon had been full of history pictures and religious compositions; in that it resembled "all previous Salons" and Baudelaire ended his review with this wish: "May the true seekers give us next year the most unusual pleasure of celebrating the appearance of something new!"

As it turned out, what was new in 1846 was not so much Delacroix's painting as Baudelaire's definition of modern art. Modern art meant Romanticism, and this Romanticism lay "neither in the choice of subjects nor in exact truthfulness, but in the artist's way of feeling." The artist can "make the Romans and Greeks into romantics if he is one himself." One can understand then how it was that, in Baudelaire's eyes, Delacroix had become "the head of the modern school" and "the latest expression of progress in art."

In order to make clear what he meant by this new way of seeing and feeling, the critic did not limit himself to a review of the single group of pictures exhibited by Delacroix in 1846—The Abduction of Rebecca (from Ivanhoe), The Farewell of Romeo and Juliet, Marguerite in Church (from Goethe's Faust), and a watercolor Lion. He made a searching retrospective survey of Delacroix's career. In particular Baudelaire recalled the sarcasm and abuse provoked in 1822 by Dante and Virgil in the Inferno, a picture ridiculed by Delécluze as a "daub." As against this blind hostility he pointed to the enthusiastic and prophetic article written by Thiers, then a young journalist (later famous as a statesman and historian), which he quoted at length— thus providing some support for those who have claimed that Baudelaire was not the only 19th-century art critic to have spoken aptly and admiringly of Delacroix.

Eugène Delacroix (1798-1863).
Scenes of the Massacres at Chios, 1824. Oil painting.
Louvre, Paris.

Pages 50-52: Details.

After a biographical sketch, Baudelaire went on to define the "principal characteristics of the great painter," the first of which was his "universality." "Delacroix is universal. He has painted genre pictures full of intimacy, and historical pictures full of grandeur. He alone perhaps, in our unbelieving century, has conceived religious pictures which were neither cold nor empty like competition pieces, nor pedantic, mystical or neo-Christian, like the works of all those philosophers of art who treat religion like an archaistic science and think it necessary above all else to master the symbols and traditions of the early church before they can strike the proper religious note." In proof of this Baudelaire cited Delacroix's Pietà in the Paris church of Saint-Denis du Saint-Sacrement, in front of which he had paused so often:

"The majestic queen of sorrows is holding on her knees the body of her dead son, her arms outstretched horizontally in a fit of despair, a mother's paroxysm of grief... The group is spaced out and disposed entirely against a uniform dark green background, which might be taken either for a mass of boulders or a storm-tossed sea. This background is fantastic in its very simplicity; Delacroix, like Michelangelo, has doubtless suppressed the accessories in order not to dim the clarity of his conception. This masterpiece leaves on the mind a deep furrow of melancholy."

Melancholy: another great quality of Delacroix's, "the most remarkable of all his qualities, and one that makes him the true painter of the nineteenth century—that singular and persistent melancholy which emanates from all his works, and which is conveyed by the choice of subjects, by the expression of faces, by the gestures, and by the style of the color." Nothing surprising then in the fact that Delacroix preferred Dante and Shakespeare to all other poets: "two other great painters of human sorrow." As he looked back over the whole sequence of Delacroix's pictures, Baudelaire wrote: "It is as if one were watching the celebration of some painful mystery." "In several of them, by some recurring play of chance, we find one figure more stricken and crushed than the others, one figure which sums up all the surrounding grief; such is the woman with her hair hanging down, kneeling in the foreground of the Crusaders at Constantinople; such is the old woman, so forlorn and wizened, in the Massacres at Chios."

This emphasis on the painful side of his painting was not entirely to the liking of Delacroix, who felt that Baudelaire exaggerated his melancholy and morbidity. The poet, however, whose words applied as much to himself as to the pictures he was reviewing, went even further in his Salon of 1859 and above all in the obituary he wrote after Delacroix's death in 1863, whose tenor may be seen from the following extract: "His work is all desolation, massacres, fires; everything in it bears witness to man's eternal and incorrigible barbarity. Burnt and smoking cities, slaughtered victims, ravished women, the very children cast beneath the horses' hoofs or under the dagger of distracted mothers; his whole work, I say, is like a terrible hymn composed in honor of fatality and irremediable pain."

George Catlin (1796-1872). Stumich-a-Sucks or Buffalo Bull's Back Fat, 1832. Oil painting.
National Collection of Fine Arts, Smithsonian Institution, Washington, D.C.

Among the colorists who, while hardly in the same class with Delacroix, nevertheless commanded attention by their forceful temperament and originality, Baudelaire singled out two: Catlin and Decamps. George Catlin was an American artist who in the 1830's had spent eight years with Indian tribes in the Far West, painting hundreds of pictures of Indian life. Two of his Indian portraits were shown in Paris at the 1846 Salon. They were ignored by most critics but Baudelaire was struck by them: "Catlin has rendered superlatively well the proud free character and noble expression of these splendid fellows... With their fine attitudes and easy movements, these savages make antique sculpture comprehensible. As for the coloring, there is something mysterious about it that delights me more than I can say."

Decamps was a French artist who had traveled widely in the Middle East and specialized in scenes of Oriental life. Baudelaire shared his contemporaries' admiration for Decamps, who today is unjustly neglected. He was one of those, wrote Baudelaire, "who for many years now have tyrannically held the public's interest, and rightly so. Gifted with a marvelous power of analysis, this artist has often achieved powerful results by a happy combination of small devices. If he shirked linear detail too much, often contenting himself with movement and outline, and if his drawing occasionally verged on stylishness, yet his careful rendering of nature, studied above all in its light effects, always kept him safe and sustained his work on a high plane."

Alexandre Decamps (1803-1860).
Schoolroom in Asia Minor. Oil painting.
Municipal Museum, Amsterdam.

Ary Scheffer, the "ape of sentiment," was the typical eclectic. "An eclectic is one who does not know that an artist's first concern is to substitute man for nature and so to challenge nature." Instead of concentrating on painting, "which is only made interesting by qualities of color and form," Scheffer relied continually on the help of the other arts, especially poetry. "A ridiculous blunder for two reasons: first of all, poetry is not the painter's immediate aim; when it is mixed with painting, the work is all the better for it, but poetry cannot mask the shortcomings of a work. To make a point of looking for poetry in the conception of a picture is the surest means of not finding it. It must come without the artist's being aware of it."

Ary Scheffer (1795-1858). St Augustine and St Monica, 1854. Oil painting. By Courtesy of the Trustees, National Gallery, London.

Jean-Dominique Ingres (1780-1867). Cherubini and the Muse of Lyric Poetry, 1842. Oil painting. Louvre, Paris.

After Delacroix, it was Ingres who occupied "the most important place." He was the great master of line, of that highly personal line which summed up both "the ideal and the model," for if it is not to lapse into naturalism line must idealize its subject. The ideal is "the individual rectified by the individual." In his sketches Ingres "draws with a natural eye for the ideal; his drawing... does not contain many strokes; but each stroke renders an important contour." And though he does not know how to compose pictures, "his portraits are almost pictures, in other words intimate poems."

Nicolas-Toussaint Charlet (1792-1845).
"Maybe that's how we'll be
next Sunday!" 1832. Lithograph.

The cover of the Salon of 1845 *had announced the forth-coming publication of a book called* On Caricature. *This book, on which Baudelaire is known to have been working in 1847, in 1851 and again in 1853, never appeared. The gist of it, however, was incorporated in three articles:* On the Essence of Laughter and on the Comic generally in the Plastic Arts, *a kind of theoretical introduction published in July 1855 in* Le Portefeuille; *and* Some French Caricaturists *and* Some Foreign Caricaturists, *both of which appeared in October 1857 in the magazine* Le Présent. *It has been shown by Claude Pichois that in spite of their date of publication all three articles were for the most part written at the time of the first* Salons.

For Baudelaire laughter is essentially satanic because it is governed by pride. It expresses the idea of superiority, either of man over man or of man over nature. In the first case we are concerned with the significant comic, the comic of manners; in the second, with the absolute comic, the grotesque.

The best representative of the absolute comic is the German romance writer E.T.A. Hoffmann, the fantastic author of The Princess Brambilla; *in the plastic arts the absolute comic is attained only by Goya.*

In France, "land of clear thinking and demonstration, where art aims naturally and directly at utility, the comic is generally significant." See Molière or Voltaire; only Rabelais attains the grotesque.

The most powerful of French caricaturists is undoubtedly Daumier, to whom Baudelaire rightly devotes half his essay; with prophetic intuition (for at the time Daumier was disgracefully underrated) Baudelaire placed him on the same level as Ingres and Delacroix. "I want to speak now of one of the most important men, I will not say only in caricature, but in the whole of modern art... To appreciate him properly, it is necessary to analyze him both from the artistic and the moral point of view. What distinguishes Daumier as an artist is his sureness of touch. He draws like the great masters... As a moralist, Daumier has something in common with Molière. Like him, he goes straight to the point. The idea is made clear at once... His caricature is formidable in its range, but without rancor or malice. Through all his work there runs an undercurrent of decency and kindliness... One word more. What enhances the remarkable character of Daumier's work and makes him an unusual artist who belongs to the illustrious family of the masters, is that his drawing is naturally colorful."

Among the other French caricaturists, Baudelaire spoke with sympathy and discrimination of Carle Vernet, Pigal, Trimolet, Traviès and Jacque, but he denounced with ruthless lucidity the shortcomings and foibles of the most popular draftsmen of the day—Charlet, Gavarni, Grandville, Monnier. Charlet was "a slave" who "has always courted popular applause." Gavarni, creator of the Lorette, "is not essentially satirical; often he flatters instead of biting." A man of letters rather than an artist, he gives too much importance to his captions, which are "sometimes very intricate," and "he knows, as Marivaux did, the full force of understatement, which is at once a lure and a blandishment for the intelligence of the public." As for Grandville, Baudelaire respected "the lunatic side of his talent," but felt "a certain uneasiness" before his work; he was "a morbidly literary spirit, always in quest of bogus devices to force his ideas into the domain of the plastic arts."

Below:
Charles-Joseph Traviès de Villiers (1804-1859).
Mayeux, Classical Painter. Lithograph.

Gavarni (1804-1866). "Young lady, a ticket for the ball if you'll give me a kiss..." 1842. Lithograph.

Above: Jean-Ignace Grandville (1803-1847).
The Finger of God. The Louvre of the Marionnettes.
From "Un autre monde," 1844.

Below:
Gavarni (1804-1866). The Artist and his Critic. Lithograph.

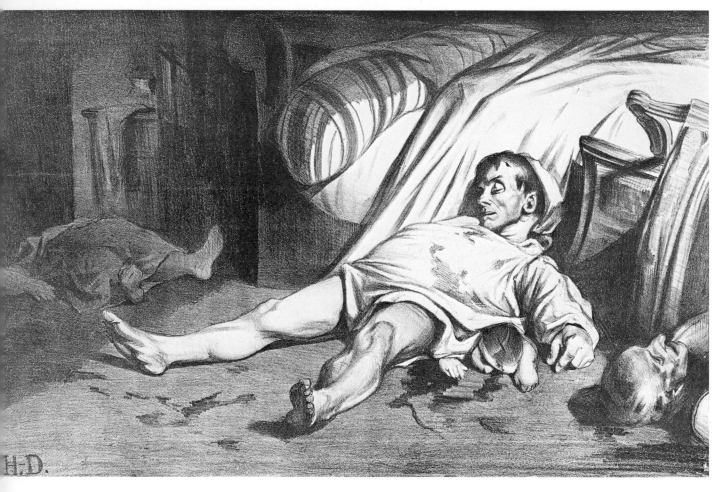

Honoré Daumier (1808-1879). Massacre in the Rue Transnonain, April 15, 1834. Lithograph.

Page 59: Honoré Daumier (1808-1879). The Artist Robert Macaire, 1838. Lithograph.

In the work of Daumier "you will see passing before your eyes, in all its fantastic and arresting reality, everything a great city contains in the way of living monstrosities. Nothing in its wealth of all that is frightening, grotesque, sinister and farcical but Daumier is familiar with it." The satirical journal La Caricature *kept up a running fire against the government. "Daumier played an important part in this endless skirmish... Over the lamentable massacre in the Rue Transnonain, Daumier proved himself a truly great artist... It is not exactly caricature, it is history, the trivial and terrible reality."*

The Robert Macaire series, wrote Baudelaire, was "the decisive starting point of the caricature of manners... It came after the bursts of revolutionary anger and drawings with topical allusions. From then on, caricature assumed a new aspect, it was no longer specifically political. It was the general satire of the people. It entered the realm of the novel."

par Mr Daumier & Philipon.   Chez Aubert gal. vero dodat   1838-184.   Imp d'Aubert et Cie

L'artiste Robert Macaire

(Bertrand, au propriétaire) C'est un fameux peintre qui s'extasie sur la beauté de votre cheval et qui demande à en faire une étude...
(Le propriétaire congratulé) très bien!! très bien!!
(Robert Macaire au propriétaire) quelle magnifique bête!! Oh! Monsieur, quelle magnifique tête vous avez!!.... permettez donc que
je complète mon étude en vous peignant à côté de votre magnifique cheval...... cela fera un tableau magnifique.....
.... Un mois après, le propriétaire reçoit une croûte vernissée, encadrée et accompagnée d'une demande de mille écus.........
il refuse de payer ce qu'il n'a pas commandé, Robert Macaire le poursuit en justice.......... il paye alors par crainte du scandale et l'artiste
passe à une autre étude.

Pieter van der Heyden (about 1530-1576?).
Patientia, 1557. Engraving after Bruegel.

William Hogarth (1697-1764).
The Reward of Cruelty, 1751. Line engraving.

George Cruikshank (1792-1878).
Very unpleasant weather, or the old saying verified:
Raining Cats, Dogs, and Pitchforks. 1835. Engraving.

The slightly shorter but perhaps even more significant study of foreign caricaturists deals with five modern artists, the Englishmen Hogarth, Seymour and Cruikshank, the Spaniard Goya, the Italian Pinelli, and one Renaissance artist, the great Flemish painter Bruegel, whose "hallucinatory" genius was rehabilitated by Baudelaire in a couple of masterly pages.

In this study Baudelaire sets out to define the specific national character of the comic in each country and the peculiar individuality of the representative artists he has chosen. His acute analysis of Hogarth's main sets of prints and of the humor of Seymour and Cruikshank reveals the poet's descriptive powers and his familiarity and understanding of the art of the print—and, it may be added, his understanding of the technique of printmaking.

His greatest praise is naturally reserved for Goya, not only because of the Spaniard's singular genius but on account of the "new horizons" he opened up in the modern domain of caricature thanks to an essentially fantastic vision. Baudelaire deserves of course less credit for glorifying Goya than for glorifying Daumier, for the series of Caprichos and Bullfights were already well known and appreciated in France and Théophile Gautier had written an enthusiastic article on them (of which Baudelaire reminded his readers). But there is a wonderful breadth and acuteness in Baudelaire's remarks on the Spanish master, who had taken his place among the Beacons.

Of Goya, he writes: "... in works that spring from profoundly individual minds there is something akin to those periodic or chronic dreams that regularly haunt our sleep. This is the mark of the true artist, who is steadfast and unchanging even in those fugitive works, that hang as it were on events, which we call caricatures. It is that mark, I say, which distinguishes historical caricaturists from artistic caricaturists, the fugitive comic from the eternal comic." Goya possessed "a love of the ungraspable, a feeling for violent contrasts, for the staggering horrors of nature and for human faces strangely animalized by circumstances," but he always contrived to "make the monstrous credible." With him, "art is at once transcendental and natural," so that "the line of junction between the real and the fantastic is impossible to grasp."

Francisco Goya (1746-1828).
"And still they do not go!" (¡Y aún no se van!), 1797. Etching.

Gustave Courbet (1819-1877). Portrait of Baudelaire, 1847. Oil painting. Musée Fabre, Montpellier.

The Literature of Commitment

The childish utopia
of the *art for art's sake* school,
by excluding morality,
and often passion too,
was necessarily barren.

THE best portrait we have of Baudelaire as a young man was penned by himself in *La Fanfarlo*, a short story published in 1847—the only one he ever wrote, for *The Young Charmer* was adapted from an English original. There Baudelaire, as if foretelling his own future, takes leave of his hero with these words: "Poor Manuela de Monteverde! How low he has fallen! I have just heard that he has founded a socialist paper and wants to enter politics."

As a matter of fact, after making a brilliant start as an art critic, Baudelaire went through a period of uncertainty during which he revealed a political commitment that astonished his contemporaries no less than it does their descendants. What! The dandy who, in his *Salon of 1846,* had urged the police to beat up a republican, "an enemy of roses and perfumes," a "foe of luxury, literature and the arts," manned the barricades in 1848? That is where Jules Buisson saw him: "On the evening of February 24 I came across him at the Buci crossroads. He was one of a crowd who had pillaged an armorer's shop and carried a fine double-barrelled gun, brand-new and shiny as a new pin, and a magnificent bandolier in yellow leather that was no less spotless. I hailed him and he came up to me, feigning great excitement. 'I have just been in the firing line,' he said. 'You don't mean for the Republic?' I asked, looking at his brand-new artillery. To this he gave no reply but went on shouting that they had to go and shoot General Aupick. Never had I been so struck by the distressing lack of character in a man of such a noble, original nature."

But however sharp Baudelaire's animosity against his father-in-law, it is not an adequate explanation of the fact that he did take part in the revolutionary movement. He was also led to do so by reading Swedenborg, Fourier, and Proudhon. We know too that he actually approached the latter, to whom he wrote two letters in August 1848. Those sources of inspiration would seem, at first glance, very ill-matched, were we not aware of the fact that in the nineteenth century it was easy to pass from one to the other and that it was almost impossible to believe in the symbolism of flowers without, sooner or later, following the socialist lead. It is, indeed, typical of this mutual dependence of aesthetic ideas and social theories that the terms *symbolism* and *socialism* were both invented by Pierre Leroux, some of whose formulas Baudelaire occasionally took over.

The Revolution of February 1848 established the freedom of the press. This meant that anyone could set forth his opinions in a newspaper of his own. The result was that within a year more than five hundred journals appeared. One of them was *Le Salut public*, founded by Baudelaire, Champfleury and Toubin. It is hard to discover what each of the three wrote, but a violent article entitled *God's Punishments*, whose style is vaguely reminiscent of Lamennais's *Words of a Believer*, is generally attributed to Baudelaire. It portrays Louis-Philippe as "the wandering Jew of the Monarchy," who "goes from nation to nation, from town to town... He runs as fast as he can to arrive somewhere before the Republic, somewhere to rest his head. That is his dream. But no sooner does he reach the walls than the bells start ringing gaily and fill his distraught ears with the peals of the Republic."

When *Le Salut public* died for lack of funds, Baudelaire continued his career as a political journalist with *La Tribune nationale* which, just when he joined it, turned its coat from democratic and socialist to conservative. No matter. A few months later he went so far as to seek the editorship of a reactionary sheet called *Le Représentant de l'Indre*. That experience was as short-lived as the others. The poet left Châteauroux on the evening of the day he arrived after scaring the good burghers with the unpleasant witticisms he made after the banquet organized in his honor. It was no doubt with his political changes of front in mind that he later observed, in *My Heart Laid Bare*: "I have no convictions, in the sense of the word my contemporaries understand, for I have no ambition." And again: "I can understand a man's deserting a cause in order to find out what it feels like to serve another."

Baudelaire's political commitment did not survive Napoleon III's coup d'état. "December 2 depoliticized me physically," he wrote to Ancelle on March 5, 1852. His interest in Edgar Allan Poe and Joseph de Maistre helped him to revert to his aristocratic sentiments as an artist and a dandy.

Nonetheless, Baudelaire's bout of revolutionary fever left its traces in both his poetry and his critical writings. The pieces that make up the section entitled *Wine* in the *Flowers of Evil* and some other poems such as *The Ransom* celebrate work and effort and promise that those who toil will be rewarded for their labor. He wrote an amazing preface to *Songs and Ballads* by Pierre Dupont, whom he knew personally and admired for a sentimental humanism that was extremely popular in 1848. In that preface Baudelaire did not hesitate to break a lance as an artist in defense of humanitarian ethics and action, and deplore "the childish utopia of the *art for art's sake* school" of which Théophile Gautier, to whom the *Flowers of Evil* was subsequently dedicated, expounded the theory in his preface to *Mademoiselle de Maupin*. The purpose of poetry, Baudelaire said,

was to express "public sentiments"; its duty was to foster the aspirations of the collectivity. "Begone, illusive shades of René, Obermann and Werther... The spirit of action leaves you no place among us." Statements of this sort are well calculated to astonish those who recall Baudelaire's admiration for Senancour and, still more, for Chateaubriand. The latter, he said in *Fusées*, represented, on a par with Poe and Alphonse Rabbe, the "eternal note" and the "eternal, cosmopolitan style." As a matter of fact, when Baudelaire ten years later, in 1861, resumed his study of Dupont in *Reflections on Some of My Contemporaries* he took good care not to sing the praises of the lyric poet to the disadvantage of the people he really admired.

When his enthusiasm had cooled he passed a severe judgment on his political commitment: "1848 was only amusing," he wrote, "because we all built utopias like castles in Spain. 1848 was only charming because it was so excessively ridiculous." The February Revolution, like that of 1789, can be explained by man's natural taste for destruction and his inclination for evil, "the taste for vengeance, the *natural* love of destruction. Literary enthusiasm, bookish memories." In *Poor Belgium* he made a last confession: "As for *me*, when I consent to be a republican, *I do wrong and do it knowingly. Yes! Long live the Revolution!* Always! Anyhow! But I am not taken in. I have never been taken in! I say *Long Live the Revolution!* just as I might say *Long Live Destruction! Long live Expiation! Long live Punishment! Long live Death!* Not only would I gladly be a victim, I wouldn't even dislike being an executioner: to feel the Revolution from both sides! All of us have the republican spirit in our veins, as we have the pox in our bones. We are democratized and syphilized."

Gustave Courbet (1819-1877).
Preparatory Drawing for the Vignette
of "Le Salut public."

Ernest Meissonier (1815-1891). ▶
The Barricade (detail), 1848.
Oil painting. Louvre, Paris.

We can get a very good idea of what Le Salut public *was like from the memoirs of one of its three editors, Professor Charles Toubin, an enthusiastic researcher into the archaeology and folklore of his native Jura. "As soon as the provisional government [of 1848] was inaugurated, it proclaimed absolute freedom of the press: no more surety, no more censorship, no more preliminary declarations. What about founding a newspaper? Baudelaire and Champfleury asked me at once. Let us found a newspaper, I replied, since there is an absolute need for one... The title was soon chosen. Baudelaire proposed* Le Salut public. *I found it rather too fiery, but my two collaborators pointed out that when there is a Revolution one must raise one's voice if one wants to be heard. So I withdrew my objection... As for any unity of views and opinions, we didn't bother about that in the least. Champfleury had only one political idea:*

he loathed the police. Baudelaire adored the Revolution, like everything else that was violent and abnormal. For that reason I feared him more than I loved him. But I bowed to the inevitable. Courbet did a vignette for us of a working man on a barricade; I think it was engraved by Chien-Caillou (Rodolphe Bresdin). The first issue of Le Salut public *was written in less than two hours on three tables on the second floor of the Café Turlot. The second issue was produced with more care and made such a hole in our capital that we were unable to do a third. So, for us, it was a case of 'to be or not to be.' Baudelaire, for whom there were no incompatibles, presented one copy devoutly to the archbishop of Paris and took another democratically to Raspail, the revolutionary who lived on the Place de l'Ecole de Médecine and for whom he professed limitless affection and admiration after reading "The People's Friend."*

Gustave Courbet (1819-1877). A Funeral at Ornans, 1849. Oil painting. Louvre, Paris.

It is impossible to say exactly when Baudelaire first met Courbet, but it must have been at the time he published his first Salons. It was apparently in 1847 that the painter did the portrait of the poet. Their mutual friend, the essayist and novelist Champfleury who was at once the theoretician of realism and the historian of folk art, tells us that though it was a fine picture neither the artist nor his sitter was quite satisfied with it. The two of them met frequently until 1852, either in the painter's studio on the Rue de la Harpe or at the Brasserie Andler, opened in 1848 on the Rue Hautefeuille (the street in which Baudelaire was born), where the realist group forgathered.

At the Salon of 1850-1851 Courbet, who was only thirty-one at the time, exhibited a number of canvases, among them Stone Breakers and Funeral at Ornans. Théophile Silvestre reported that the pictures "were received with cries of astonishment, repugnance and admiration." These attacks led Champfleury to write an article in which he defended the right of realist art to depict life as it appears to an impartial observer. "As for the alleged ugliness of these burghers, there is nothing false or exaggerated in it; it is simple and true. It is the ugliness of the provinces, which must not be confused with the ugliness of Paris. For that matter, every age has its own beauty and the black frock

coat suits ours perfectly because we all take part in some funeral or other." And Champfleury went on to congratulate Courbet for having understood the ideas set forth in "a rare and curious book, the Salon of 1846 by M. Baudelaire," namely that "the great colorists succeed in rendering colorful a black frock coat, a white tie and a gray background." Baudelaire's eulogy on the frock coat may well have strengthened Courbet's intention to paint people in contemporary dress. But when the aesthetic of Courbet, Champfleury and their friends tended to crystallize in a realist doctrine that was increasingly narrow and aggressive, Baudelaire disassociated himself from it. All the more so because, encouraged by the example of Poe, who confirmed him in his "supernaturalism," he gave up "committed" writing in favor of an art that existed only for its own sake. However, though he never devoted a special study to Courbet—actually he did once think of compiling a catalogue of his works—Baudelaire was greatly impressed by the quality and novelty of his contribution to art. "One must do Courbet the justice of recognizing that he has done much to restore the taste for simplicity and frankness and the absolute, disinterested love for painting."

Courbet photographed by Nadar.
(Archives photographiques, Paris.)

Gustave Courbet (1819-1877).
Bunch of Asters, 1859.
Oil painting. Kunstmuseum, Basel.

M. Courbet dans toute la gloire de sa propre individualite, allégorie réelle détern in ut une phase de sa vie artistique. (Voir le programme, où il prouve victorieusement qu'il n'a jamais eu de maitre... de perspective.

Caricature of Courbet's "The Studio" by Quillenbois.
Woodcut from "L'Illustration" of July 21, 1855.

Caricature of Courbet's "The Studio."
From "Le Monde Illustré," 1862.

Courbet made Baudelaire a present of his Bunch of Asters, *a magnificent picture dedicated to the poet in memory of a visit Courbet and Alexandre Schanne paid him at Honfleur in 1859, during which they discovered Boudin together. This proves that the personal bonds that linked those two diametrically opposite temperaments were stronger than the aesthetic differences that separated them. The mutual comprehension of the poet of dandyism and the "mighty workman" of painting was stronger than any theory.*

In June 1855, after the jury of the Paris World Fair had refused a number of works he had sent in, Courbet decided to appeal directly to the public and opened a show of his own. First and foremost among the new pictures on show was The Painter's Studio, *Courbet's major work and one of the most important paintings of the mid-nineteenth century. "A real allegory that defines a phase of seven years of my artistic life," Courbet himself described it. At the far right, among the elect "who live their life," Baudelaire, absorbed in a book, represents Poetry. But his features are not those of 1855, for Courbet simply copied the likeness he had done in 1847. Beside Baudelaire is the barely visible figure of a Negress looking at herself coquettishly in a mirror. She must be Jeanne Duval whose image Baudelaire himself apparently asked the painter to remove before the show opened because he thought her vicinity would compromise him. In any case the silhouette we can still see is very like the one Baudelaire drew in 1864.*

Courbet's exhibition was violently attacked in the press. Champfleury defended it in an article-manifesto printed in L'Artiste *of September 2, 1855 ("On M. Courbet, A Letter to Madame Sand"). Baudelaire planned to write a reply both to* The Studio *and to the* Letter *stressing his own independence. Unfortunately* Since Realism Exists—*the intended title of the study—never developed beyond the stage of notes for the subject. Baudelaire would have denounced the narrowness of the doctrine upheld by Courbet, who was "contaminated" by Champfleury and his friends, and at the same time would have demonstrated that "all good poets have always been realists."*

Gustave Courbet (1819-1877). The Painter's Studio ▶
(right side), 1855. Oil painting. Louvre, Paris.

When did Baudelaire first become acquainted with Poe's writings? More important still, how far did the American poet influence the author of the Flowers of Evil? *These two questions have caused a lot of ink to flow and have not yet been settled entirely.*

Mesmeric Revelation, *the first of Poe's stories translated and annotated by Baudelaire, was printed in* La Liberté de penser *on July 15, 1848. At that time Poe was not altogether unknown in France, for adaptations of his works had already been published in 1845. But Baudelaire himself tells us—and in this he is corroborated by Asselineau— that it was Isabelle Meunier's translations, first published in* La Démocratie pacifique *in 1847, that called his attention to the American writer. In any case Baudelaire did not become more closely acquainted with them during the next few years. As W.T. Bandy has proved, his first important piece on Poe,* Edgar Allan Poe, His Life and Work *printed in March and April 1852 in the* Revue de Paris, *edited by Maxime Du Camp, was not taken from the posthumous edition published in New York in 1850. Baudelaire got his material mainly from two American newspaper articles which appeared after Poe's death and which he more than once slavishly copied. This means that it was not until after that date that Baudelaire really went into the subject of Poe, most of whose prose writings he translated—not all with equally good results—between 1852 and 1865. It is worthwhile noting that this was the part of his literary labors that brought in most money. The French edition of Poe,* Histoires extraordinaires *and* Nouvelles Histoires extraordinaires, *was at once a best seller and repeatedly reprinted.*

A real translation is an act of creation and thanks to Baudelaire Poe has come to be an author whose work, paradoxically enough, is more highly thought of in France than in the English-speaking countries. There, in fact, many critics, among them P. Mansell Jones and the poet T.S. Eliot, in an essay that created a sensation, consider that Baudelaire overrated the importance of the American author and failed to recognize his weak points.

The secret of this success and of Baudelaire's devotion to his model is that he identified himself with him. The French writer insisted on this identity and even exaggerated it. "Do you know why I translated Poe so patiently?" he wrote to Théophile Thoré *in June 1864. "It is because he was like me. The first time I opened one of his books I saw there, with dismay and delight, not only subjects I had dreamt of but also PHRASES of mine that he had written twenty years before." Which just goes to show how far Baudelaire made Poe's work his own.*

The same assimilation occurred on the biographical level. As early as 1856 Champfleury observed that Baudelaire "must have imagined more than once that he was Edgar Poe himself." In the three important studies Baudelaire devoted to Poe in 1852, 1856 and 1857 it is clear to see that the American poet is intentionally presented as a brother of his French translator. Taking as an excuse his unhappy life, Baudelaire endowed Poe with some of his own characteristics and attitudes. To write another man's biography is a good pretext for writing about oneself. Translating another man's works might also be a pretext, or an alibi, for masking one's own lack of creative power. Drawing up the balance sheet of his literary activity, in 1865, Baudelaire confessed: "I wasted a lot of time translating Edgar Poe and the great profit I got from it was that some charitable people said I borrowed from Poe poems I had written ten years before I had even heard of his works." Not ten years, as we have seen, but perhaps four or five. All the same, if Baudelaire's poetry owes little or nothing to Poe, the latter's writings helped Baudelaire, at the very time when he was becoming increasingly committed to socialist and realist literature, to rediscover and assert his true artistic ideas, namely that art is largely a conscious creation and exists only for its own sake. That is what Baudelaire meant when he said: "De Maistre and Edgar Poe taught me to think."

Poe's great merit is to have protested against "the major modern heresy: teaching." The purpose of poetry is not to prove a truth. As Baudelaire wrote in the preface to the Nouvelles Histoires extraordinaires, *"It is both by poetry and through poetry, by music and through music, that the soul glimpses the splendors beyond the tomb."*

Photograph of Edgar Allan Poe, 1848. ▶
Poe-Ingram Collection, University of Virginia Library, Charlottesville, Va.

P. 74: Baudelaire photographed by Carjat (detail), 1861-1862.

" The Flowers of Evil "

You know that I have always thought
of literature and the arts as pursuing aims
quite foreign to morality,
and that for me beauty of conception
and style is enough.

THE story of *Les Fleurs du Mal* is closely connected with the story of Baudelaire's life. The earliest poems of the collection were written when he was twenty years of age or even younger, at the time of his voyage to the Mascarenes. During his voluntary exile in Brussels at the end of his life he offered *Le Parnasse contemporain* a bouquet of *New Flowers of Evil*, which were published in 1866 just after he had lost the power of speech. So that during the whole quarter of a century covered by his literary activity Baudelaire worked on this book, one of the keystones of modern poetry.

The first public announcement of Baudelaire's intention of publishing a collection of poems appeared in 1845. On the cover of *L'Agiotage*, a satire by Pierre Dupont, an advertisement reads: "Forthcoming: *The Lesbians* by Baudelaire-Dufays."

The title *The Lesbians* is a concession to a vogue that was very widespread in France during the second third of the nineteenth century, as witnessed for instance by Henri De Latouche's *Fragoletta*, Balzac's *The Girl with Golden Eyes* and Théophile Gautier's *Mademoiselle de Maupin*. It would, however, be a mistake to believe that Baudelaire's volume would have been merely an exaltation of Sapphic love and its devotees. It would probably have included not only the poems *Women Accurst*, *Lesbos* and *Sed non satiata*, but also *The Albatross*, *The Giantess*, *Carrion*, *To a Malabar Girl*, *The Rebel*, *Bertha's Eyes*, and other pieces which, Prarond tells us, Baudelaire recited to his friends as early as 1843.

At the end of 1848 the title of the projected book was changed from *The Lesbians* to *Limbo*. "I am fond of mysterious titles and titles that make a bang," Baudelaire once confessed to his publisher Poulet-Malassis. *The Lesbians* may be said to come under the second of these categories, *Limbo* under the first. In what sense should we take the new title? Has it a theological, Fourierist or Dantesque significance? "They are no doubt socialist poems and therefore bad poems," surmised a contemporary critic. But the sense in which Baudelaire himself uses the word *limbo* sets us on a different track. Referring, in his *Salon of 1846*, to "the singular and persistent melancholy" that made Delacroix "the true painter of the nineteenth century," he observed that it "pervades even *Women of Algiers*, the most elegant and florid of his pictures. This little poem of an interior, all quiet and silence... breathes the indefinable, heady perfume of an evil haunt, which leads us soon enough towards the bottomless limbo of melancholy." So, in Baudelaire's eyes, the word limbo meant the region in the vicinity of Hell that Dante visited in Virgil's company in the fourth Canto of the *Inferno*, which in fact is quoted in the *Salon of 1846*.

One is confirmed in this impression on reading the eleven poems published under the title *Limbo* in *Le Messager de l'Assemblée* on April 9, 1851. Three entitled *Spleen* frame one called *The Ideal*, and are followed by *Death of Artists* and *Death of Lovers*, until finally, in *The Owls*, we reach the conclusion Pascal reached two centuries earlier, namely that we owe all our troubles to the fact that we cannot stay in our room at home. We are told in a note that these poems are taken from a book that will soon be published "and intends to tell the story of the spiritual unrest of modern youth."

The writing of the book was probably well advanced at that time. In fact Baudelaire was already handing his poems to a copyist and Asselineau saw the precious manuscript in the poet's home bound in two quarto volumes. It has never been found.

In 1852 Baudelaire gave up the idea of taking *Limbo* as the title of his work; *Les Fleurs du Mal* was definitely chosen in 1855. Tradition has it that it was not Baudelaire's own invention but was suggested by his friend Hippolyte Babou during a conversation in a café. This title first appears over the eighteen poems he published in the *Revue des Deux Mondes* of June 1, 1855. They included a number of poems inspired by Madame Sabatier, among them *Dawn and the Spirit*, *Reversibility* and *Confession*. They were pervaded by a Petrarchesque mysticism and restored in favor of the Ideal a balance that *Limbo* had caused to lean too far toward Spleen.

At that point the main lines of the future collection were established, though some sections are still missing—for instance, *Wine*, *Revolt* and *Death*—and the poems do not follow each other in very strict order.

This order, which was established *a posteriori* after all the poems were written, is very important. A fact stressed by Barbey d'Aurevilly who, in his review of the first edition of the *Flowers of Evil*, said: "We cannot, even if we wanted to, quote any of the poems in this collection and this is the reason why: the piece quoted would be judged solely on its own merits but, and one must not miss this point, in M. Baudelaire's book every poem has, over and above the felicitous details or the well-found idea, *a very important value as part of a sequence occupying a certain position*, which one must not deprive it of by isolating it from the rest. Artists who know how to see lines under the splendor and beauty of the colors will perceive very clearly that here the poet has intentionally thought out a secret architecture, a well-calculated plan."

Baudelaire used this architecture as an argument in his favor when he was prosecuted in 1857 for offending public morals by the hypocritical justice of the Second Empire. He insisted that his book should be judged as a whole but his plea was rejected and he was forced to suppress six of the poems.

Had it not been for this sentence, would Baudelaire have gone back to work on the volume? Some things he said lead one to doubt it. For instance: "And those confounded *Flowers of Evil* that I have to start working on again! One needs tranquillity for that. To go back and be a poet, artificially, by an act of the will; to get back into a rut one thought was dug once and for all; to take up again a subject one thought was finished and done with; and all this to obey the whim of three magistrates!"

But instead of replacing six poems, he wrote thirty-five. He revised the whole book and added a new section called *Parisian Tableaux*, consisting of pieces whose forthright modernism leads straight to the *Short Prose Poems*. On January 1, 1861, he wrote to his mother: "For the first time I am almost satisfied. The book is *almost good*; it will endure as testimony of my disgust and my hatred of all things."

The arrangement of the second edition of 1861 is far more strict than that of the first. "The only praise I want for this book is the recognition that it is not a mere album but has a beginning and an end. All the new poems were written with a view to fitting them into the peculiar framework I had chosen," Baudelaire told Alfred de Vigny in December 1861.

The edition of 1861 is the last that the poet was able to revise himself. The third, published in 1868, was edited by Asselineau and Banville, who inserted in the section entitled *Spleen and Ideal* a score of poems they had discovered in manuscript inserted in Baudelaire's copy of the second edition. This gives it a purely documentary value.

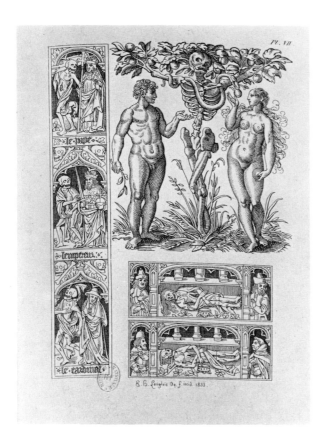

16th-century woodcut reproduced in "Essai sur les danses des morts" by Eustache-Hyacinthe Langlois.

In the Flowers of Evil, *as in a collection of baroque poems, the dominant idea is the idea of death:*

Death can console, and Death can re-create;
Life's hope and goal, which, as strong liquors might,
Arouse our courage and intoxicate,
And give us heart to walk until the night.

This idea decided the choice of the engraving Baudelaire wanted for the frontispiece of the second edition of his book. This is how he explained his plan to Nadar in 1859: "Here a skeleton that forms a tree with the legs and ribs for the trunk, the outstretched arms sprouting the leaves of poisonous

plants in rows of little pots arranged as in a greenhouse. The idea occurred to me as I was leafing through Hyacinthe Langlois's *Dances of Death.*"

To realize this plan Baudelaire had in mind a German engraver, perhaps even Alfred Rethel, and two Frenchmen, Célestin Nanteuil and Penguilly-L'Haridon, both of whom were outstanding book illustrators of the romantic period. He did not want Gustave Doré because, he said, his figures "always have something childish about them."

In the end his choice fell on Félix Bracquemond, very likely on the recommendation of Poulet-Malassis, who was a friend of his. But Bracquemond's taste clashed with Baudelaire's. After a number of trial sketches—the poet scribbled some rude remarks on one of them—they gave up the idea of a symbolic frontispiece and decided on a portrait of Baudelaire engraved by Bracquemond. Later, in Belgium, Baudelaire asked Félicien Rops for a frontispiece which was used for Les Epaves.

The series of Flowers of Evil *is brought to a close by a sequence of poems grouped under the title* Death. *This ending is carefully prepared for all through the collection and is foreshadowed by pieces like* Carrion, The Pull of the Void, Burial, The Digger Skeleton, Dance of Death, Fanciful Engraving *and many others.*

The last three of the poems named above were inspired by works of art. Baudelaire often based his poems not on a slice of life, an actual situation, but on reality that had already been purified in the crucible of art. This act of creation at one remove enabled him to achieve a higher, longer flight. In Dance of Death, *dedicated to Ernest Christophe, he took his inspiration from a statuette by that sculptor which he had seen at the 1859 Salon. This is how he described the work:* "Imagine a big female skeleton all ready to go to a ball. The face, flattened like that of a negress, the lipless, gumless smile, the gaze which is nothing but a hole full of darkness, make this horrible thing that was once a beautiful woman look as if she was vaguely searching in empty space the delicious hour of the love tryst or the solemn hour of the witches sabbath recorded on the invisible dial of the centuries. The bust, eaten away by time, rises coquettishly from the bodice like a withered bouquet from its wrappings, and the whole funereal conception stands erect on the pedestal of a pompous crinoline. To cut the story short I should like to quote a rhymed fragment in which I have attempted to explain, not to illustrate, the subtle pleasure this little figure gives...*

As proud as one alive of her fine bearing,
With scarf, and gloves, and big bouquet of flowers,
She has the nonchalance, the easy daring,
Of slim coquettes deploying all their powers."

Page 78:
Projected Frontispiece by Bracquemond
for "Les Fleurs du Mal," 1860.
Etching with annotations by Baudelaire.
Daniel Sicklès Collection, Paris.

Ernest Christophe (1827-1892).
The Dance of Death, about 1859.

FANCIFUL ENGRAVING

For all costume, the freakish specter wears,
Upon his bony brow, with rakish airs,
A paste-stone diadem in ghastly taste,
Whipless and spurless, galloping posthaste
A ghostly nag of the apocalypse
Whose epileptic nose flares wide and drips.
Together deeper into space they bore,
On heedless hoofs the infinite to explore.
The horseman waves a sword with flaming blade
Above the vague crowds trampled by his jade;
And, like a prince inspecting his household,
Moves on through graveyards, endless, bare, and cold,
Where, under pale white sunlight, peoples lie
Of ancient and of modern history.

English translation by Francis Duke
reprinted by courtesy of the
University of Virginia Press

Death on a Pale Horse, 1784. Etching by Haynes after John Hamilton Mortimer, illustrating the Apocalypse (VI, 8).

THE DUEL

Two warriors fell on one another; arms
Spattered the air with blood, and din, and flashes.
Those shocks, that din, those thunderous alarms,
Were those of youth that in its first love thrashes.

The blades are broken — like our springtime life,
My love! But still, our claws and teeth can yet
Do better than the sword or treacherous knife.
O fury of seasoned hearts by love beset!

Into a gorge where pards and panthers thresh,
Our heroes rolled, locked in a grim embrace,
And the bare brambles bloomed with bits of flesh.

That gorge is Hell; the beast, the human race!
We too must roll, inhuman Amazon,
So that our hatred's ardor may blaze on!

English translation by Francis Duke
reprinted by courtesy of the
University of Virginia Press

Francisco Goya (1746-1828). "Who would have believed it!" (¡Quien lo creyera!), 1797. Etching.

Auguste Clésinger (1814-1883). Woman Bitten by a Snake and Bust of Madame Sabatier, 1846. Marble. Louvre, Paris.

In Spleen and Ideal, *the first section of* Flowers of Evil, *the cycle of the Black Venus inspired by Jeanne Duval contrasts with the cycle of the White Venus which assembles the poems written in honor of Madame Sabatier. She was a lady of easy virtue, famous among writers and artists, and a life-size bust and nude of her exhibited by the sculptor Clésinger at the 1847 Salon were a great success. Between 1852 and 1854 Baudelaire dedicated to her a whole series of poems:* To One Too Gay, Reversibility, Confession, The Living Torch, Dawn and the Spirit, "What will you say tonight, poor solitary soul..." *and* Hymn, *but did not sign them. On May 8, 1854, he wrote to her as follows: "For me you are not only the most attractive of women, of all women, but also the dearest and the most precious of superstitions." At the time of the trial her mystical devotee was identified at last and she yielded to him. This is the harrowing confession the Angel who had fallen from her heavenly pedestal received next day: "A few days ago you were a goddess, something so convenient, so beautiful, so inviolable. Now you are a woman."*

TO ONE TOO GAY

Your head, your gestures, and your air
All share a rural landscape's grace,
And laughter plays about your face
Like breezes when the skies are fair.

As you brush past, your touch disarms
The surliest stranger, by the health
That bursts in all its dazzling wealth
Out of your shoulders and your arms.

The brilliant hues and joyous fancies
Which enliven your attire
Set every poet's dreams afire
With images of flower dances.

Mad frocks only indicate
Your spirit's bubbling gaiety;
O madcap who have maddened me,
My love is equalled by my hate!

I strolled one day, dull and depressed,
Along a garden's grassy way;
And felt the sun's ironic ray
That tore a path into my breast;

And Springtime's verdant opulence
Had left me so humiliated
That, raging, I decapitated
Flowers, for Nature's insolence.

Just so, I'd like, some evening soon,
When Pleasure's silken hour has rung,
Towards your body lithe and young
To creep in silence, vile poltroon,

Your joyous flesh to wound and slash,
Your breast in pardon to chastise,
And, to your thunderstruck surprise,
Cut in your side a gaping gash;

Then, to my peak of joy to win,
As soon as those new lips unfold,
Redder and fairer than the old,
My sister, pour my poison in!

English translation by Francis Duke
reprinted by courtesy of the
University of Virginia Press

THE MASK

ALLEGORICAL STATUE
IN THE RENAISSANCE MANNER

To Ernest Christophe, statuary

Let us admire this graceful Florentine
Whose body's muscles, in their undulation,
Strength, and his sister Elegance, enshrine.
This woman, this miraculous creation,
Robust and delicate in equal measure,
Might rule soft couches, and give inspiration
To pontiffs or to princes in their leisure.

Thus, note the smile, thin heady invitation
To rapt Fatuity's ecstatic gaze;
The look, dry, mocking, measured, indolent;
The small pert features lost in gauzy haze,
Each of which tells us, proudly confident:
"By Pleasure I am ruled, by Love I'm crowned!"
In this bright creature, then, what charms abide!
What gentleness of character is found!
But now to see her from her other side.

O blasphemy of art! O dread surprise!
From that fair body's promise of content,
Two monstrous heads on shapely shoulders rise!

Yet no! the mask is merely fraudulent
Of features lit by that fine-drawn grimace,
For now behold, atrociously distorted,
The veritable head, the natural face,
Behind the other, spurious face contorted!
Poor beauty, whose great stream of tears has burst,
And drowned my heart beneath its inundation,
I love your lie, and quench my parching thirst
In the deep waters of your Tribulation!

Why should that beauty weep, of such perfections
That she might bind the human race in chains?
Whence come her wasting and obscure infections?

She weeps, you fool, at having known life's pains!
At knowing them today! But her most sorrow,
At which her shudders shake her to the knee,
Is that, alas, she still must live tomorrow!
And on — like us — into eternity!

English translation by Francis Duke
reprinted by courtesy of the
University of Virginia Press

Ernest Christophe (1827-1892). The Mask (detail). Marble. Garden of the Tuileries, Paris.

Ch. Baudelaire

Hauteville House — 30 août 1857

J'ai reçu, Monsieur, votre noble lettre et votre beau livre. L'art est comme l'azur; c'est le champ infini. Vous venez de le prouver. Vos Fleurs du Mal rayonnent et éblouissent comme des étoiles. Continuez. Je crie bravo de toutes mes forces à votre vigoureux esprit. Permettez-moi de finir ces quelques lignes par une félicitation. Une des rares décorations que le régime actuel peut accorder, vous venez de la recevoir. Ce qu'il appelle sa justice vous a condamné au nom de ce qu'il appelle sa morale. C'est là une couronne de plus.

Je vous serre la main, poète.

Victor Hugo

Baudelaire already enjoyed a legendary reputation before 1857, but the publication of the Flowers of Evil *added fuel to the fire that fed it. It was apparently Gustave Bourdin who first called the attention of the law to the immortal work by a review in* Le Figaro *that was both stupid and censorious: "The hateful and the filthy stand cheek by jowl; the loathsome and the corrupt go hand in hand. Never before have we seen so many breasts nibbled and gnawed in so few pages; never before have we witnessed such a review of demons, embryos, devils, chloroses, cats and vermin." Bourdin, in righteous indignation, goes on to conclude that "nothing can justify a man over thirty years of age giving publicity in a book to such horrors."*

Baudelaire was to a considerable extent consciously responsible for the legend whose victim he finally became. From Brussels he complained to Ancelle on October 13, 1864, that "a lot of people crowded round the author of the Flowers of Evil *with all an idler's curiosity. The author of those* Flowers *could be nothing if not a monstrous eccentric. All that rabble thought I was a monster and when they saw that I was cool, collected and polite—and that I abhorred free thinkers, progress and all idiotic modern ideas—they decreed (I suppose) that I was not the author of my book... What a comical way of confusing the author with the subject! So the confounded book (of which I am very proud) really is obscure and incomprehensible! I shall long pay the penalty for daring to portray evil with a certain talent." However, another letter, written to Madame Paul Meurice on January 3, 1865, proves that Baudelaire found it hard to resist the temptation to astonish fools and preen himself in front of idlers: "I swim in dishonor like a fish in water." But journalists and critics were not the only people who were eager to spread Baudelaire's legend. Caricaturists too*

◄ Caricature of Baudelaire by Eugène Giraud, after 1862. Pencil and watercolor, based on a photograph by Carjat. Mrs Ronald Davis Collection, Paris.

◄ Letter from Victor Hugo to Baudelaire, dated August 30, 1857. Bibliothèque Historique de la Ville de Paris.

Page 92: Baudelaire photographed by Carjat, about 1863.

were anxious not to miss so choice a target. Even Nadar, though he was one of the poet's most faithful friends, did not scorn to achieve a facile effect. About 1858 he took up the caricature he had done in 1855 for his Panthéon Nadar *and embellished it with a carrion. Marcelin, in* Le Monde illustré *of January 30, 1858, drew Baudelaire as a baby with a depraved expression "sniffing a bouquet of* Flowers of Evil." *Eugène Giraud, in a caricature after Carjat's famous photograph, gave the poet the dull, fixed gaze of a drug addict. Emile Durandeau, who had published in 1857 an "Odyssey of Pilou, Fusilier in the 73rd Regiment of the Line," reworked one of his drawings turning Pilou into a poet. As a result on July 15, 1858,* Le Journal inutile *introduced its readers to a Baudelaire whose bed had just been overturned by a horrible orgy; the caricature bore the caption: "Oh! c'est beau de l'air!"—a pun on the poet's name. The same drawing, embellished with new details, appeared in* Le Boulevard *of December 1, 1861, under the title "The Nights of Monsieur Baudelaire" with a commentary by Théodore de Banville: "A truckle-bed, a beam, a rag-bag, a death's head, a retort, an ibis, a rag, a he-goat, a trunk, a rat, a broom, a cat, the devil as the cat's shadow, a hovel that would scare the bad woman named Veronique! What powerful, double-triggered irony. In fact one should read* The Nights of Monsieur Baudelaire *as they are imagined by the fossilized* rentiers *of the* Rue Cocatrix, *who think Maître Marie is a* woman lawyer *and George Sand a cavalry officer. For the lucky people who had the privilege to be on intimate terms with Charles Baudelaire nothing in the world is more ridiculous than to see confined in this rag-picker alchemist's hovel a poet so infatuated with dandyism and politeness that he could say of himself: 'My soul takes wing on perfume as other men's on music.' Like Edgar Poe, who owes it to him that he exists for us, the poet of the* Flowers of Evil *knows how to draw tender music from the strings of pain and melancholy; but like Poe too, and perhaps to a still higher degree, he has the most delicate, the grandest feeling for the* home, *for the quiet, sensuous pleasure of the most ideal elegance. All the same, Emile Durandeau was right to put him in his fanciful lumber-room: it is a masterpiece of antiphrasis, which of all sorts of humor is the most forceful and enjoyable."*

Romantic Art

What does pure art
mean from the modern point of view?
It means creating a suggestive magic
containing both object and subject,
both the world outside the artist
and the artist himself.

GENERAL Aupick died on April 28, 1857, in the reign of Napoleon III who had appointed him Ambassador successively to Constantinople and Madrid and finally made him a Senator. So he did not live to see his stepson prosecuted for offending against public morals. His death quickened the poet's filial piety and at the same time laid upon him a duty which he had no intention of evading. On June 3, 1857, Baudelaire wrote to his mother: "For me this occurrence was something solemn, like a call to order. There have been times when I was very harsh and rude to you, my poor mother; but, after all, I could consider that someone had made it his business to make you happy—and the first idea that struck me on his death was that from now on it was naturally my business to do so."

The poet had been in love with Madame Sabatier for several years and that love came to a head in August of the same year, at the very time of the *Flowers of Evil* trial. Madame Sabatier's Sunday dinners were attended by the most prominent artists and writers of the day, such as Préault, Meissonier, Clésinger, Gautier, Feydeau, Dumas the elder, Flaubert, Bouilhet, Maxime Du Camp, Berlioz, Delacroix. But not everybody appreciated the atmosphere in her house. For instance, the Goncourts made the following entry in their *Journal* for April 16, 1864: "Spent the evening with Madame Sabatier, on whom Clésinger modeled his Bacchante. She is a fine figure of a woman with a common hearty way, a rather vulgar courtesan. This rather coarse old-style beauty is my idea of a vivandière." (The last sentence was added by Edmond de Goncourt in 1887.)

Between 1852 and 1854 Baudelaire had sent Madame Sabatier a number of poems, some of them accompanied by unsigned letters in a disguised hand.

She must have pretty soon discovered the secret of her mysterious devotee, for some of the poems he sent her were printed in magazines before the *Flowers of Evil* was published. Nonetheless, the first time Baudelaire wrote to her in his normal hand was when he asked her to plead with the judges on his behalf.

Despite the pain and sorrow she felt when the poet broke with her, Madame Sabatier always remained his friend and counsellor. But in reality she thought he had given her up for Jeanne Duval. In her copy of *Flowers of Evil* she kept a portrait of the mulatto woman drawn by Baudelaire, on which she had written as a caption: "His Ideal!" Actually she was mistaken. Baudelaire had left Jeanne the year before and if he visited her now and then it was because he felt that he was under an obligation to his "daughter," as he called her from then on, toward whom he played "the part of papa and guardian."

Consequently, when the *Flowers of Evil* was published in 1857 Baudelaire was very much alone. On the other hand, most of his important works were already on the stocks by then or were started shortly after. As a matter of fact, for Baudelaire the next three or four years were a period of the greatest fertility. His creative activity, which was already immense between 1842 and 1846, slowed down during the next twelve years as a result of his political commitment and the discovery of Poe, only to reach a new peak between 1858 and 1861.

As early as February 1858 Baudelaire formed plans to leave Paris, escape from his creditors and settle in his mother's house at Honfleur on the Channel coast. This is what he wrote her at that time: "I am sincerely anxious to be far away from this wretched city, where I have suffered so greatly and wasted so much time. Who knows but my spirit may grow young again down there in quiet and happiness? — In my head I have a score of novels and two plays. I want much more than an honest, vulgar reputation; I want to overwhelm men's minds, astonish them like Byron, Balzac or Chateaubriand." But he postponed his departure from one week to the next despite the good advice he gave himself in his *Journaux intimes* and his good intentions of following Flaubert's example of hard-working solitude.

In January 1859, at long last, he took the plunge and settled down to work as soon as he reached Honfleur. There he wrote a number of new *Flowers* that he judged "passably singular." They included *Dance of Death* and *Travel*, a "long poem dedicated to Maxime Du Camp, apt to make nature shudder and lovers of progress still more." Its dedication to the author of *Chants modernes*—the first of which begins with a line that runs: "I am a traveler born..."—was somewhat ironical. Indeed Baudelaire foresaw the dedicatee's surprise, for he wrote: "If the systematically Byronic tone of this little poem displeases you and if you are shocked, for instance by my making fun of progress or because the Traveler says he saw nothing but triviality, or indeed for any other reason, do not scruple to tell me so." It was at Honfleur, where he found his "fluency" again, that Baudelaire wrote his important study of Théophile Gautier and his *Salon of 1859*. It was there too that he revised the second part of his *Artificial Paradises*, on opium and its effects.

In spite of all this we find Baudelaire back in the blazing heat of Paris in June 1859. He was drawn back to the capital by the need to see his friends again and more especially by his literary interests. In fact, the latter were not very flourishing. And it was in vain that he tried to find a publisher for his literary and artistic criticism. Finally, on January 1, 1860, he sold his *Literary Opinions* and *Aesthetic Curiosities*, together with *Artificial Paradises* and the second edition of *Flowers of Evil* to Poulet-Malassis. But the latter's financial situation was so calamitous that he was unable to publish those works. Baudelaire's creditors gave him no respite and he was so short of funds that he was tempted to kill himself.

He wrote to Poulet-Malassis in March 1861: "For quite some time I have been on the point of committing suicide. What has stayed my hand has nothing to do with cowardice or even regret; it is pride that prevents me from leaving my affairs in a muddle. *I shall leave enough to pay*... Particularly during the last two months I have fallen into an alarming state of atony and desperation. I have suffered the same sort of malady as Gérard [de Nerval], namely the fear of being unable to think any more or write another line. It is only during the last four or five days that I have succeeded in proving that I wasn't dead in that way. That's an important point."

Poulet-Malassis went bankrupt at the end of 1862, thus putting an end to Baudelaire's hopes of seeing his critical articles published in book form. This was done after his death by Asselineau and Banville. Yet those articles are no less important than his poems in prose and verse, nor less modern. As Georges Poulet has pointed out, Baudelaire's criticism involved his identifying himself with his subject. "If you want to give a good idea of a work," Baudelaire wrote in his first article on Pierre Dupont, "you must *get inside the skin* of the fictitious character, become impregnated completely with the feelings he expresses, and feel them so deeply that you have the impression that the work is your own. To render a work properly you have to assimilate it."

Eugène Delacroix (1798-1863). Ovid in Exile among the Scythians, 1859. Oil painting.
By Courtesy of the Trustees, National Gallery, London.

Baudelaire gave up art criticism to a certain extent after the Salon of 1846. His poetry and still more his work as a journalist and translator prevented him from writing regular reviews of the exhibitions held in the Louvre. It was with the greatest difficulty that he found time, in connection with the Paris World's Fair of 1855, to extol the diametrically opposite qualities of Ingres and Delacroix, more amply and in greater detail than he had done in the Classical Museum of the Bonne-Nouvelle Bazaar. *In his introduction, he repeated his profession of faith as a critic; he insisted on the importance of achieving "the divine grace of cosmopolitanism" which "so few men possess completely," and made a violent attack on "the idea of progress, that ridiculous idea that flourishes on the rotten soil of modern fatuity."*

The Salon of 1859 *was written at Honfleur, the haven by the sea where Baudelaire's mother had waited for him in vain for so many years. In a letter to Nadar on May 14, 1859, he said: "Just now I am writing about a Salon that I did not see. But I have a catalogue. Guessing at the pictures is a tiring job, but otherwise it is an excellent method and I recommend it to you. One is afraid of being too generous with praise and blame. The result is impartiality." It was certainly an original exercise and well suited to a man who took imagination, "the queen of faculties," as the keystone of his aesthetic system. "It was imagination," he said, "that taught man the moral significance of colors, contours, sounds and scents. At the beginning of the world it created analogy and metaphor. It decomposes all creation and, with the materials piled up and arranged in obedience to laws whose origin can only be found in the deepest depths of the soul, it creates a new world and produces the sensation of something new."*

This paean in praise of imagination, which alone enables us to penetrate the web of analogies that links impressions to feelings and ideas, led him inevitably to condemn without appeal the realist doctrine that Courbet, Champfleury and Duranty had championed in recent years. For all realism degenerates into verism and "here the exclusive love of Truth (so noble when limited to its proper applications) crushes and stifles the love of Beauty."

By the same token, the most dangerous enemy of painting is photography. "I am convinced," Baudelaire said, "that the ill-applied advances of photography, like all other purely material progress, has done much to impoverish the French artistic genius, which was already so rare." The sole purpose of photography is to be the humble handmaiden of the arts and sciences—a purely documentary function. Let it not encroach "on the domain of the intangible and the imaginary, on all that owes its value to the fact that man has projected his spirit into it."

These are the criteria on which Baudelaire judged the pictures he reviewed. First and best of all, Delacroix. "What an imagination Delacroix has! It has never hesitated to scale the perilous heights of religion. It has conquered heaven, hell, war, Olympus, sensuality. He is the prototype of the painter-poet!"

And he went on to extol at considerable length Delacroix's picture of Ovid in Exile *among the Scythians: "There, on wild greenery, with a womanly indolence and melancholy, lies the celebrated poet who taught the art of love. Will his powerful friends in Rome succeed in overcoming the imperial rancor? Will he ever return to the sumptuous pleasures of the prodigious city? No, from this inglorious land the long, melancholy stream of the* Tristia *will flow in vain; here he will live and here he will die."*

Truly imaginative artists like Delacroix realize that "nature is nothing but a dictionary . . . There one looks up the meaning of words, the formation of words; there one finds all the elements that make up a phrase or a story; but no one has ever viewed a dictionary as a composition in the poetical sense of the word. Painters who follow their imagination look in their dictionary for the elements that match their idea; by adapting them with a certain art they give them an entirely new look. Those who have no imagination copy the dictionary."

That is why Théodore Rousseau, though Baudelaire praised him highly in his Salon of 1845, *is inferior to Corot. Rousseau "falls a victim to the famous modern defect that springs from a blind love of nature, but of nature alone: he mistakes a simple study for a composition." Corot, instead, "is one of the few, perhaps the only one, who still has a strong feeling for construction, who observes the relative value of each detail in the whole!"*

In the long chapter of his Salon of 1859 *which he devoted to landscape painting, Baudelaire extolled the fantastic talent of the engraver Charles Meryon, who gave a visionary quality to the topographical details of a Paris in the throes of a complete transformation. And he added a special paragraph on Eugène Boudin, the precursor of the Impressionists whom he had recently met at Honfleur and whom he praised for his "meteorological beauties" and his "prodigious air and water magic."*

This splendid Salon of 1859, *which reveals Baudelaire's critical genius at full maturity, also includes an important though seldom quoted study on sculpture, in which he sets forth with great discernment the essential qualities of sculpture and the "divine role" that the meticulous knickknackery of the period too often failed to fulfill.*

Camille Corot (1796-1875).
Landscape with Figures or The Toilet, 1859. Oil painting.
Private Collection, Paris.

Théodore Rousseau (1812-1867).
The Gorges of Aspremont at Fontainebleau, before 1859.
Oil painting. Middlebury College Collection, Middlebury, Vermont.

François-Joseph Heim
(1787-1865).
Portrait of Delacroix,
1858. Black chalk.
Louvre, Paris.

Paul Baudry (1828-1886). The Penitent Magdalen, 1858.
Oil painting. Musée des Beaux-Arts, Nantes.

Eugène Fromentin (1820-1876).
A Street at El Aghouat. Oil painting.
Musée Municipal, Douai.

Armand Gautier (1825-1894).
The Sisters of Charity, 1859. Oil painting.
Palais des Beaux-Arts, Lille.

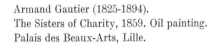

Octave Penguilly-L'Haridon (1811-1870).
The Seagulls. Oil painting.
Musée des Beaux-Arts, Rennes.

Eugène Boudin (1824-1898)
Cloudy Sky. Pastel.
Louvre, Paris.

Constantin Guys (1802-1892).
Two Spanish Women on their Balcony. Black wash.
Musée des Arts Décoratifs, Paris.

Baudelaire's essay on The Painter of Modern Life *was published in* Le Figaro *in November and December 1863, but he had written it between 1859 and 1860. Like the studies on humor and the caricaturists, the pages on Constantin Guys, the "painter of modern life," were apparently excerpts from a large-scale work that Baudelaire planned to devote to* The Painters of Manners, *in which he would have presented a whole series of minor artists of the eighteenth and nineteenth centuries. Of this vast project only a few notes have been preserved.*

Some authors have regretted that Baudelaire chose Guys, undoubtedly a gifted painter but not a genius, as a basis for his theory of modernity. They cannot have realized that what Baudelaire needed was not so much a model as a pretext, and that at the outset he placed Guys among the minor artists, like Gavarni, Devéria and Traviès, who are chiefly interesting because they show us "circumstantial beauties and details of manners."

In fact, Baudelaire seized every chance to expand his discourse and develop points of general aesthetic interest. Thus the sketches of an English draughtsman offered him a pretext to expound his idea of the dual nature of beauty: "Beauty consists of an eternal, invariable factor, the quantity of which is extremely difficult to determine, and a relative, circumstantial factor, which may be—one at a time or all together—the period, fashion, morals or passion. Were it not for this second factor, which is like the amusing, titillating, appetizing wrapping of the divine cake, the first would be indigestible, unpalatable, unsuited and unfitted for human nature." Modernity is precisely this transitory, fleeting, contingent factor.

Baudelaire frequently went so far as to identify himself with Guys. He lent him his own preferences, obsessions and passions, particularly in the chapters devoted to the dandy, to the praise of makeup, to the artist as a man of the crowd. "The crowd is his element, as air is the bird's or water the fish's. His passion and his profession consist in espousing the crowd. The perfect idler, the impassioned observer finds immense pleasure in merging with the undulating, flowing, transient, infinite crowd. To be away from home, yet feel everywhere at home; to see the world, be in the hub of the world, yet be hidden from the world. These are among

Constantin Guys (1802-1892). The Champs-Elysées. Brown wash and watercolor. Musée du Petit Palais, Paris.

the lesser pleasures of those independent, impassioned, impartial spirits that the language lacks the resources to define exactly. The observer is a prince who has the privilege of being incognito everywhere. Those who love life take the whole world as their family, just as those who love women make room in their family for all the beauties they find, might find or cannot find ; as those who love pictures live in a charmed company of dreams painted on canvas. In the same way those who love universal life dive into the crowd as into a huge reservoir of electricity." There could be no better commentary on some of Baudelaire's poetic compositions, such as Crowds in his Short Prose Poems.

Victor Hugo and Théophile Gautier caricatured by Nadar.
Preparatory drawings for the Pantheon, 1851-1852. Bibliothèque Nationale, Paris.

Gustave Flaubert caricatured by Eugène Giraud. Bibliothèque Nationale, Paris.

Baudelaire is often extolled as the first art critic of his day. This admiration is undoubtedly justified but, when intended in the narrowest sense of the term, it detracts from his merits on two counts. In fact, Baudelaire was not the only art critic of outstanding talent and intuition: Thiers when a young man, Planche and Thoré-Bürger proved no less shrewd on many occasions. Nor must it be forgotten that Baudelaire was not merely an art critic. He wrote no less admirably on Flaubert than on Delacroix, on Gautier and Banville than on Constantin Guys; not to mention his pages on Wagner. Baudelaire always took up a clear position in relation to the artists and writers of his day.

His first essays in literary criticism date back to the time of his first Salons. *He started out with anonymous contributions to* Le Tintamarre *and* Les Mystères galans des Théâtres de Paris *and flattering or spiteful reviews and humorous essays in* Le Corsaire-Satan. *His short-lived enthusiasm for*

democratic and republican ideas next led him to take up political journalism and socialistic criticism. For a few years he was an active supporter of useful art and the identity of Beauty, Truth and Good. But the example of Edgar Allan Poe and Joseph de Maistre helped him to discover an aesthetic more suited to his romantic temperament. In fact, his true gods were Chateaubriand, Hugo, Balzac, Flaubert, Gautier, and even such "minor Romantics" as Alphonse Rabbe and Petrus Borel.

Some people have expressed their surprise that Baudelaire dedicated Les Fleurs du Mal *to the author of* Emaux et Camées, *with whom he was probably acquainted since 1843 and to whom he also devoted two critical studies. For the first of these he asked Victor Hugo to pen a preface in the form of a letter; it contains Hugo's famous tribute to the* Flowers of Evil *as giving the reader a* frisson nouveau, *a new thrill. In the first study of Gautier, Baudelaire made* the following admission: "With regard to the writer who is the subject of this article and whose name has served as a pretext for my critical observations, I may confess confidentially that I know the gaps in his astonishing intellect." As for those "gaps," they are easy to guess even though he does not pinpoint them: Gautier, as a feuilleton writer, produced too much too fast. But of Albertus, The Comedy of Death and España, Baudelaire said: "There is not a single man of letters nor an artist who is also a dreamer, whose memory is not furnished and adorned with these marvels." This is amply borne out by the many reminiscences of Gautier in the Flowers of Evil and by what Baudelaire said of Emaux et Camées, "that series of little poems of a few stanzas each, those erotic or dreamy interludes, some of which resemble sculptures, others flowers, others again jewels, but all have a color finer and more brilliant than the colors of China or India, and all have a shape purer and more precise than objects in marble or crystal. Everyone who loves poetry knows them by heart." But Baudelaire's loyalty to Romanticism never made him lose his clarity of vision. Witness his judgments on Victor Hugo. "My aim," he wrote one day to Hugo, "was to remind the reader of that wonderful literary period whose true king you were and which lives on in my mind as a delicious childhood memory." That was the time when Baudelaire was at school and asked his mother to send him Le Dernier Jour d'un Condamné. It was the time when Les Voix intérieures, Ruy Blas and Les Rayons et les Ombres were published. "Only Victor Hugo's plays and poems and one book by Sainte-Beuve (Volupté) amused me," he wrote to his mother on August 3, 1838, in a letter in which he attacked the sham brilliance of modern literature and Eugène Sue's books in particular. Since then, however, Hugo had been converted to Democracy and Progress. In exile on the Channel island of Jersey he posed as a seer and claimed a priestly mission; he saw himself as Prometheus and "sets an imaginary vulture on his breast, which is tortured only by the stings of vanity." Nonetheless, La Légende des Siècles is still a very fine book though tainted by some modern follies. As for Les Misérables, Baudelaire wrote to his mother: "This book is disgusting and absurd. I have proved, in this connection, that I have mastered the art of lying." The lies in question took the shape of a review which is one of the best analyses of "the spirit of charity" that pervades Hugo's great novel. But despite the compassion he feels for the weak and the outcast, the critic still believes that art's function is not to place itself at the service of a humanitarian ideal. "A work of art should have no other aim but art." Hugo thanked Baudelaire in a letter that the latter found "absolutely ridiculous... It shows that a great man can be a fool." Baudelaire had already proved that one does not have to esteem a man very highly to appreciate his works at their true value.

Théodore de Banville. Drawing by Alfred Dehodencq. Bibliothèque Nationale, Paris.

Honoré Daumier (1808-1879).
Hashish Smokers, 1845. Lithograph.

Baudelaire started taking an interest in drugs in the days of his gilded youth. There was nothing original in his curiosity, which was shared by most romantic writers, such as Nodier, Balzac, Gautier, Vigny and Flaubert. He had his first taste of opium at the Hôtel Pimodan, or perhaps even earlier at Louis Ménard's. Be that as it may, the experiments of the too famous "Hashish Club" described by Théophile Gautier did not go very far and were, in fact, carried out under medical control. Dr Moreau, of Tours, was not sorry to take advantage of the reactions of a few artists for the scholarly analyses he published in his Hashish and Mental Derangement in 1845. Baudelaire's own first essay, Wine and Hashish compared as Means for the Multiplication of the Personality, published in 1851,

was prudent and schoolmasterly. As a physiologist, he extolled wine and disparaged hemp. The same "moderate socialism" inspired the poems of the section entitled Wine in Flowers of Evil, which probably dates from the same period or thereabouts.

When, less than ten years later, Baudelaire took up the problem again he did so as a poet who had long been addicted to opium in the shape of medicinal laudanum. By then he had had the good fortune to find in Thomas De Quincey a catalyst of his ideas, as Poe and Delacroix had been at an earlier date.

The second part of Artificial Paradises takes the form of a thyrsus in which Baudelaire's meditations are intimately and inextricably blended with the Confessions of an English Opium-Eater. There the poet again condemns the use of drugs, not in the name of a half-baked humanitarianism, but because "man is forbidden, at the risk of decadence and intellectual death, to alter the primordial conditions of his existence and disturb the balance between his faculties and the environment in which they are destined to function, in short, to interfere with his destiny and replace it with a new sort of fatality."

As it happens, this urge to violate and transgress the laws of his condition is in the noble nature of man; it is man's "sense of infinity" going on the wrong track. In fact, "it is this corruption of the sense of infinity that, as I see it, is the cause of all culpable excesses, from the solitary, concentrated intoxication of the writer, who is forced to resort to opium for relief in physical pain and, having found there a source of morbid pleasure, makes it by degrees his sole hygiene and, so to say, the sun of his spiritual life, to the most repulsive drunkenness of the slumdweller, who rolls ridiculously in the filthy streets, his brain alight with fire and glory."

Baudelaire compares the intoxication produced by drugs with the rapture one feels on contemplating Delacroix's pictures, listening to Wagner's music, reading Banville's poems, or writing a poem oneself. But, unlike these licit pleasures, artificial intoxication is sterile and, what is worse still, it disintegrates the personality. All the same, if Baudelaire condemns drugs, he does so with generosity and regret, as Racine condemns Phedra and Laclos condemns La Merteuil.

Baudelaire: Self-Portrait, about 1844. Watercolor. Collection of Baronne de Goldschmidt-Rothschild, Paris.

Page 106: Honoré Daumier (1808-1879). The Mountebanks Changing Place, about 1865. Pen, ink and wash. Courtesy, Wadsworth Atheneum, Hartford, Connecticut. The Ella Gallup and Mary Catlin Sumner Collection.

"Short Prose Poems"

The making of these little trifles
is the result of great mental concentration.
I hope, however, I shall succeed
in producing a singular piece of work,
more singular, more wayward at least,
than the Flowers of Evil,
one in which the frightening is
combined with the comic,
and even tenderness with hatred.

FLOWERS OF EVIL was not just the first collection of modern poetry; it was also the end-product of a poetic tradition dating back some three centuries. There can be little doubt that Baudelaire became most clearly aware of the limitations imposed on him by regular verse forms, when he was preparing the second edition of the *Flowers* and particularly when he was composing the admirable poems that make up the core of the *Parisian Tableaux*. *The Swan* and *The Little Old Women*, for example, conjure up the daily reality of the capital in a manner appreciably different from that of the two *Twilight* poems: the vocabulary is more varied, more colloquial, and certain deliberately bare lines come very close to prose. However, in dealing with prosaic subjects, it was not sufficient to "depoeticize" the verse. The confrontation with a new world, dedicated to the cult of Progress, demanded a new kind of poetry.

There seemed to be two possible approaches: to follow the example of Leconte de Lisle in his *Poèmes antiques*, or to write *Chants modernes* in the manner of Maxime Du Camp. The poet could either turn his back on modern life or sing the praises of the steam-engine in old-fashioned Alexandrines. Baudelaire found a solution to the problem, however, by inventing an instrument that permitted him both to protest against the absence of poetry in the modern world and to demonstrate the beauty of that world.

Baudelaire's experiments in the field of the prose poem began about 1855, or even earlier, and consist of transpositions into prose of pieces in verse. Examples are to be found in *La Fanfarlo* and *On Wine and Hashish*. Such "doublets" also feature in the *Prose Poems*, in which Baudelaire more than once deliberately used themes already dealt with in the *Flowers of Evil*.

This repetition of themes is of some importance, since Baudelaire intended the *Prose Poems* as a "pendant" to *Flowers of Evil*. "In short, it is *Flowers of Evil* over again, but with much more freedom, detail, and irony." His desire for freedom and irony dictated his choice of prose, which alone permitted "that argumentative tone, that sarcasm and humor, which poetry repudiates and which constitute a kind of discord, an outrage to the idea of pure beauty."

But of what did this prose consist? Baudelaire defined it thus in his Dedication to Arsène Houssaye: "A poetic prose, musical without rhythm or rhyme, flexible and abrupt enough to adapt itself to the lyrical impulses of the soul, to the twists and turns of reverie, and to sudden onsets of awareness." This is certainly "poetic prose," but of a kind that is poles apart from the lyrical prose of Fénelon's *Télémaque*, of Rousseau, Chateaubriand, or Maurice de Guérin. Its determinedly prosaic, colloquial side has something in common with the prose of Aloysius Bertrand, which Baudelaire also evokes in the same Dedication. "I was leafing through Bertrand's famous *Gaspard de la Nuit* for at least the twentieth time, when I suddenly had the idea of attempting something of the same type and of applying to the description of modern life, or rather of *one* modern, more abstract life, the procedure he applied to his portrayal of the life of the past with its strange picturesque quality."

But as soon as he set to work, he perceived that he was doing "something singularly different" from Bertrand's vignettes of medieval life in the romantic manner of the 1830's, since he had chosen to deal with the modern world. Thus, when he sang the praises of *Good Dogs*, he refused to invoke "that old prude," "the academic muse," preferring "the familiar, city-dwelling, living muse."

In the *Short Prose Poems*, Baudelaire hoped to produce another *Joseph Delorme*—"a Joseph Delorme who strolls along, rhapsodizing over every chance encounter and drawing a disagreeable moral from everything." Like Constantin Guys, the painter of modern life, Baudelaire, the poet of modern life, aimed at creating a poetry of the commonplace. In his *Prose Poems*, which Claudel described as a singular mixture "of the Racinian style and of the journalistic style of his period," he made deliberate use of the prevailing clichés of the day. Thus, the theme of *The Old Mountebank* was one that had wide currency in art—finding its finest expression in Daumier's works—and had been popularized by the music-halls. *The Wild Woman* was a familiar figure to everyone with a taste for fairground scenes. *The Temptations* recalls a song by Paul de Kock. *Invitation to a Journey* borrowed its "blue dahlia" from a refrain by Pierre Dupont and its "black tulip" from a novel by Alexandre Dumas the Elder. In *The Parisian Prowler* and *The Solitary Walker* —other titles that Baudelaire considered for his collection—the commonplace is charged with powerful poetic overtones. "In certain almost supernatural states of mind, the depth of life is revealed in its entirety in the scene before one's eyes, however banal it may be. *It becomes its symbol.*" These words from *Fusées* are a perfect definition of the poetics of *Short Prose Poems*.

Gustave Bourdin, the hostile critic of *Flowers of Evil*, wrote as follows about this new and revolutionary work in the *Figaro* of February 7, 1864: "In the prose work, as in the work in verse, every suggestion of the streets, the atmosphere, and the sky of Paris, all the sudden onsets of awareness, all the ramifications of reverie, philosophy, dreams, and even anecdotes can take their place in turn. It is simply a matter of finding a prose that can adapt itself to the various states of mind of the melancholy stroller." When this passage is compared with the Dedication of the prose poems to Arsène Houssaye, it is difficult not to conclude that it was inspired, if not actually written, by the poet himself.

Would Baudelaire ultimately have kept the title *The Spleen of Paris* for his prose poems? It scarcely does justice to the variety of a book that contains, in addition to typically Parisian poems, pieces whose inspiration owes nothing to the capital. The abundance of forms, indeed of genres, is no less wide. Side by side with pieces that, in their lucidity and lyricism, answer to our conception of the prose poem, there are tales, short stories, fables, and "moral legends." Moreover, Baudelaire had proposed to divide these poems into various "categories," such as "Parisian things," "symbols and moralities," "dream pieces," and others. Nevertheless, the title *The Spleen of Paris*, if not definitive, reminds us that the conception of these prose poems was bound up with a state of mind, a sensibility, and a way of life that were the prerogative of the capital. From the time of his departure from Paris, Baudelaire had a presentiment that his work would remain unfinished: "A *hundred painstaking trifles*," he wrote from Brussels to Sainte-Beuve on May 4, 1865, "demanding a constant good humor (a good humor that is needed even in dealing with sad subjects), a strange kind of excitement that craves for shows, crowds, music, even street-lamps—that is what I wished to achieve! I have only got as far as *sixty*, and I cannot go any farther. I am in need of that famous *immersion in the multitude*, with whose incorrectness you were so justly shocked."

Johan Barthold Jongkind (1819-1891). The Entrance of the Port of Honfleur, 1864. Etching.

"The Port." Autograph manuscript of the prose poem published in the "Nouvelle Revue de Paris," December 25, 1864.
Bibliothèque Jacques Doucet, Paris.

Le port

Un port est un séjour charmant pour
une âme fatiguée des luttes de la vie.
L'ampleur du ciel, l'architecture mobile
des nuages, les colorations changeantes
de la mer, le scintillement des phares
sont un prisme merveilleusement propre
à amuser les yeux sans les lasser. Les
formes élancées des navires, au gréement
compliqué, auxquels la houle imprime
des oscillations harmonieuses, servent
à entretenir dans l'âme le goût du
rythme et de la beauté. Et puis surtout,
il y a ~~une~~ une sorte de plaisir
mystérieux et aristocratique pour celui
qui ~~a ~~ n'a plus ni curiosité
ni ambition, à contempler, couché dans
le belvédère, ou accoudé sur le môle,
tous ces mouvements de ceux qui
partent et de ceux qui reviennent,
de ceux qui ont encore la force de
vouloir, le désir de voyager ou
de s'enrichir.

EACH HIS CHIMERA

Under a great gray sky, in a great dusty plain, with no roads, no grass, not a thistle, not a nettle, I met several men who were walking with a stoop.

Each of them carried on his back an enormous Chimera, as heavy as a sack of flour or coal, or the equipment of a Roman soldier.

But the monstrous beast was not a dead weight; on the contrary, it enveloped and oppressed the man with its elastic and powerful muscles; with its two huge claws it clung to the chest of its mount; and its fabulous head rose over the man's brow like one of those horrible helmets with which ancient warriors hoped to strike terror into the enemy.

I questioned one of these men, and I asked him where they were going in this wise. He told me that he did not know, neither he nor the others knew; but that evidently they were going somewhere, since they were impelled by an invincible need to go on walking.

An odd thing to note: none of these travelers seemed angry with the wild beast hanging at his neck and sticking to his back; it was as if he considered it a part of himself. None of these tired, earnest faces showed any trace of despair; under the splenetic dome of the sky, their feet buried in the dust of a soil as bleak as that sky, they were going their way with the resigned countenance of those who are condemned always to hope.

And the procession passed close beside me and disappeared into the atmosphere of the horizon, at the spot where the rounded surface of the planet eludes the curiosity of the human eye.

And for a few moments I went on stubbornly trying to fathom the mystery; but soon irresistible indifference laid hold of me, and I was more heavily burdened with it than they were themselves with their crushing Chimeras.

Francisco Goya (1746-1828). "You who are at the end of your tether..." (Tu que no puedes), 1797. Etching.

Edouard Manet (1832-1883).
Portrait of Baudelaire,
1862-1868. Etching.

Edouard Manet (1832-1883).
Concert at the Tuileries,
1862. Oil painting.
By Courtesy of the Trustees,
National Gallery, London.

It is difficult to sum up in a few lines the complex and too often misrepresented relationship between Baudelaire and Manet from 1858 onwards. Himself of an earlier generation that was dominated by Delacroix, Baudelaire nevertheless always encouraged his young friend, offering him sympathy and advice. Manet engraved a portrait of Poe for him in 1859, and included him in the first really modern picture, a picture that perhaps was painted at Baudelaire's suggestion: Concert at the Tuileries. Round about the same time, Manet painted the unique and magnificent portrait of Jeanne Duval, and he etched two splendid portraits of the poet, one in 1862 and the other in 1865. In 1862, Baudelaire wrote his famous quatrain on Lola de Valence, which was inscribed on the frame and printed on the engraving of the work, and in the same year he stressed Manet's originality

Edouard Manet (1832-1883). Sketch for Olympia. Engraving.
Bibliothèque Nationale, Paris.

Letter from Manet to Baudelaire, 1865.
Daniel Sicklès Collection, Paris.

in his study on Painters and Etchers. *In February 1864
he dedicated one of his short prose poems,* The Rope, *to
Manet; this was inspired by the suicide of Alexandre, the
model for Manet's* Child with Cherries *and* Urchin with a
Dog. *In the summer of the same year, when he was in
Belgium and moving away from art criticism, Baudelaire
wrote to Thoré defending the painter in the most vigorous
terms. In April 1865, when the* Olympia *scandal broke out
at the Salon and Manet complained of the poet's absence
from Paris, Baudelaire replied to him from Brussels to
say that geniuses before him had suffered the same fate
with greater fortitude and, while comforting him, let fly
this shaft, whose full significance is well worth pondering:
"You are only the first in the decrepitude of your art."
In 1866 Nadar related that, when he visited Baudelaire at
the nursing-home in Chaillot, the poet, who had lost the
power of speech, recovered it sufficiently to pronounce three
times, in a somewhat anxious way, the two syllables of
Manet's name.*

Page 116:
Hôtel du Grand Miroir, Brussels.

Exile and Death

I long for absolute rest and unending night.
Poet of the mad delights of wine and opium,
I thirst for a liquor unknown on earth,
one that the pharmaceutics of heaven itself
could not give me;
a liquor containing neither vitality nor death,
neither stimulus nor nothingness.

BAUDELAIRE's reputation was definitely sanctioned by the publication, in 1861, of the second edition of *Flowers of Evil*. Asselineau has left us an unusually serene portrait of the poet about that time. "When the second edition of *Flowers of Evil* appeared, one may say that Baudelaire was at the height of his fame. The sharp, unjust attacks made on the book when it first appeared were not repeated. Those initial attacks had turned to the advantage of both the author and the work, for resistance to them had consolidated its success. Those who saw Baudelaire at that moment of his life, smiling, fresh, still young despite his long, graying locks, were able to realize that time and the vogue he had achieved had had a salutary, soothing effect. Old enmities were appeased and new, young sympathies reached out towards him. When he went out on the boulevard in the late afternoon, his path was lined with outstretched hands; he shook them all, proportioning his exquisite politeness to the degree of familiarity or friendship. Under this impression of general benevolence the bitterness and suspicion of his youth had melted away. He had become not only indulgent but debonair, patient with fools and contradictors. To one and all he was a charming conversationalist, good-natured, suggestive, jolly, harmless to all and a paternal counsellor for the young."

Can the man described by Asselineau be the same who, perhaps at that very time, noted in *Fusées*: "Lots of friends, lots of gloves—for fear of the mange"? Or again: "When I have inspired universal disgust and horror I shall have achieved solitude." It may be a case of misleading appearances on the one hand and systematic disparagement on the other. Be that as it may, the fact is that in a very few months Baudelaire produced, in rapid succession, some of his major works: the important study on *Richard Wagner and Tannhäuser in Paris*, several sets of *Short Prose Poems* published in young Catulle Mendès's *Revue Fantaisiste* and in *La Presse*, and his outstanding *Reflections on Some of My Contemporaries*.

Is it surprising that so active a poet thought of submitting his candidature to the French Academy? Eager to demonstrate at last his middle-class respectability, Baudelaire had to choose between the seats of Scribe and Lacordaire. In December 1861 he opted for the second "because he was a churchman and a *Romantic*." His candidature caused a stir in the press. As a result his friends, particularly Sainte-Beuve and Vigny on whom he had called, advised him to withdraw. He did so on February 10, 1862.

Meanwhile he had had serious trouble with his health. Very early in 1862 he suffered a sort of concussion, which has left its traces even in his *Fusées*. "I have nurtured my hysteria with enjoyment and terror. Now I am always dizzy, and today January 23, 1862, I had a singular warning: I felt pass over me the fluttering wing of imbecility." This premonition was soon confirmed: Baudelaire found it increasingly difficult to work. The long obituary article entitled *The Life and Work of Eugène Delacroix* which was published in *L'Opinion nationale* from September to November 1863 consists largely of passages taken from the *Salon of 1859*.

Yet Baudelaire had no lack of plans in mind. Chief among them a book about himself, *My Heart Laid Bare*, which he had been thinking of writing for years and in which he wanted to vent all his spleen. "Ah! If that one is ever published it will put the *Confessions of J.-J.* [Jean-Jacques Rousseau] in the shade." And further on: "Well! yes, the book I have dreamt of so long will be a book of grudges. I shall certainly not offend my mother or my stepfather either. But when I tell the story of my education, how my ideas and feelings were shaped, I want to make it clear that I feel cut off from the world and its affairs. I shall turn my very real gift of impertinence against *the whole of France*. I need revenge as an exhausted man needs a bath... Of course, I shall not publish *My Heart Laid Bare* until I have enough capital to take refuge outside France if that is necessary."

This letter is dated June 5, 1863. Two months later Baudelaire announced his intention of leaving Paris and going to Belgium on "a trip lasting two or three months for the particular purpose of visiting the country's *rich private galleries* and making a book out of [his] personal impressions." But the plan came up against innumerable obstacles, most of them due to the poet's habit of procrastination. Then it underwent a change: the picture galleries were ousted in favor of a series of articles for *L'Indépendance belge* and of lectures at the Brussels Art Club. However, Baudelaire's real aim was to sell his collected works to Victor Hugo's wealthy publisher, Lacroix.

On April 24, 1864, Baudelaire reached Brussels at long last and put up at the Hôtel du Grand Miroir, where he spent two of the last years of his life in a shabby room on the second floor overlooking the courtyard. The hotel, which was demolished in 1959, was situated on a little street called Rue de la Montagne that rises gently towards the cathedral of Sainte-Gudule. In May and June Baudelaire delivered five lectures at the Club on Delacroix, Gautier, and his own *Artificial Paradises*. They were not very successful and the fee he received was less than he had been promised. It was then that he started making notes for a pamphlet against Belgium, which in his eyes was merely a caricature of middle-class, Voltairian France. "What a mob of rascals! I thought that France was an absolutely barbarous country, but I must admit that there is a country still more barbarous than France! After all, whether my debts force me to stay here or I make my escape to Honfleur, I shall finish this little book, which has at least made me sharpen my claws. I shall use them later on against France. This is the first time I have had to write a completely humorous book, at once comic and serious, in which I have to talk about all sorts of things. It means getting away from modern stupidity. Perhaps I shall be understood at last!"

But it was no use. Baudelaire collected his material and toured the chief provinces of the country, but his book would not take shape and his notes for *Poor Belgium* rarely rise above the level of invective. His health, too, got worse and in March 1866 he had a stroke of paralysis and lost the power of speech. His mother and Arthur Stevens brought him back to Paris on July 2, 1866, and placed him in Dr Duval's clinic, where he died on August 31, 1867, without recovering his speech.

Mallarmé had written in *L'Artiste* of February 1, 1865: "In winter, when I am weary of my torpor, I immerse myself with delight in the pages of *Flowers of Evil* I love so well. No sooner have I opened my Baudelaire than I am drawn into an amazing landscape that lives before my eyes with the same intensity as those conjured up from the depths by opium." And on November 16 of the same year Verlaine noted in *L'Art:* "What, in my eyes, makes Charles Baudelaire so profoundly original is that he represents forcefully and essentially modern man... as the excessive refinements of civilization have made him."

Les yeux de Berthe

Vous pouvez mépriser les yeux les plus célèbres,
Beaux yeux de mon enfant, par où filtre et s'enfuit
Je ne sais quoi de bon, de doux comme la Nuit!
Beaux yeux, versez sur moi vos charmantes ténèbres!

Grands yeux de mon enfant, arcanes adorés,
Vous ressemblez beaucoup à ces grottes magiques
Où derrière l'amas des ombres léthargiques,
Scintillent vaguement des trésors ignorés.

Mon enfant a des yeux obscurs, profonds et vastes
Comme toi, Nuit immense, éclairés comme toi!
Leurs feux sont ces pensers d'Amour mêlés de Foi
Qui pétillent au fond, voluptueux ou chastes.

LES BELGES ET LA LUNE

On n'a jamais connu de race si baroque
Que ces Belges. Devant le joli, le charmant,
Ils roulent de gros yeux et grognent sourdement.
Tout ce qui réjouit nos cœurs mortels les choque.

Dites un mot plaisant, et leur œil devient gris
Et terne comme l'œil d'un poisson qu'on fait frire;
Une histoire touchante; ils éclatent de rire,
Pour faire voir qu'ils ont parfaitement compris.

Comme l'esprit, ils ont en horreur les lumières;
Parfois sous la clarté calme du firmament,
J'en ai vu, qui rongés d'un bizarre tourment,

Dans l'horreur de la fange et du vomissement,
Et gorgés jusqu'aux dents de genièvre et de bières,
Aboyaient à la Lune, assis sur leurs derrières.

The rough draft of Poor Belgium fills some three hundred and sixty pages and their perusal leaves the reader with an unpleasant impression. One can hardly stand so much anger and hate that lack any real target and merely reflect the poet's unhappy state at the time he wrote them. The only interesting items are those that concern art. Not contemporary art, for in Baudelaire's view all Belgian painters except Félicien Rops and Alfred Stevens were "imitators" and "understudies of French talents." Nor ancient Flemish painting which, he said, "only distinguishes itself by qualities that are far from intellectual" and reveals "no spirit but sometimes a rich coloring and nearly always an amazing manual skill." What, instead, found favor in his eyes was Belgian Baroque, a "misunderstood style" whose merits he resolved to extol.

The churches in Brussels, Malines, Antwerp and Namur have a peculiar richness, "part curios, part junk." What caught Baudelaire's fancy was not only the architecture of those monuments as a whole but, in particular, the pulpits, confessionals and other furnishings. "Jesuit decoration has something of the theater and something of the boudoir," he wrote. Often a Jesuit church is, so to say, "centered in the pulpit"—those "huge, theatrical pulpits" that are "a mass of emblems, a pompous medley of religious symbols," covered with "palm trees, oxen, eagles, griffins; Sin, Death, round-cheeked angels, the instruments of the Passion, Adam and Eve, the Crucifix, foliage, rocks, curtains, etc., etc." The confessionals are no less rich: some are "pompous," some "dramatic," some merely "charming," but all of them are characterized by the "religious coquettishness" that makes Jesuit churches the "boudoirs of Religion."

Page 120: Baudelaire with a Cigar
photographed by Charles Neyt, Brussels 1864.

Page 121: "Bertha's Eyes."
Pen drawing by Baudelaire, Brussels 1864.

Pulpit in the Cathedral of Saint-Rombaut at Malines, Belgium.

Of all the baroque churches that he visited in Belgium, the one Baudelaire liked best by far was Saint-Loup at Namur, "the masterpiece of Jesuit masterpieces." Besides, Namur was "neglected by tourists" because "the donkey guides don't mention it." One reason more for Baudelaire to dwell on it. "The birthplace of Boileau and Vandermeulen," he observed. "The impression of Boileau and Vandermeulen remained with me during my entire stay. And, after I had visited its monuments, the impression of Lecterns. At Namur all the monuments date from Louis XIV, or Louis XV at the latest." There are three important churches: The Recollects, Saint-Aubin and Saint-Loup. It was with regard to them that Baudelaire wanted to "define, once and for all, the beauty of this style" that is still misunderstood, a "style of genius," as he did not hesitate to call it, "ambiguous and complex, elegant and awe-inspiring." He planned to give a "technical description (as far as possible)." Begun in 1621 under the supervision of Pierre Huyssens, Saint-Loup was different from any other Jesuit church Baudelaire had seen. The black stone that adorns the capitals of the columns and the arches gives a somber impression. There is none of the agreeable "whiteness" that had pleased him in the church of John the Baptist in the Beguine convent. "The Beguine church in Brussels is a girl making her first communion. Saint-Loup is an awe-inspiring, delightful catafalque." It is a "sinister and gallant prodigy." And when the sun shines through the stained-glass windows the interior is like a "catafalque embroidered in black, rose and silver." Baudelaire returned to Namur several times to admire this edifice of which, he said, he never tired. He made his last trip there with the painter Félicien Rops in mid-March 1866. It was at that time, in the church of Saint-Loup itself, that he had the fall from which he was never to recover.

Confessional in the Church
of Saint-Loup at Namur, Belgium.

Interior of the Church of Saint-Loup ▶
at Namur, Belgium, about 1860.
Lithograph by F. Stroobant.

CRITICAL ESSAY BY GEORGES POULET

BAUDELAIRE AND THE REAL WORLD

I Baudelaire, who am I? To this question, which the poet continually asked himself, the immediate reply, always the same, was this: I am a man; that is a fallen being, ashamed to exist, doing evil, treading on dirt which is no different from myself. Moreover, in my wretchedness and vileness, I discover myself to be a poet. But a poet does not belong to a different species from other men. He simply happens to be a man whose repulsiveness—a characteristic common to all men—stands out more sharply than anyone else's and inspires in others, at first sight, a keener feeling of horror. I Baudelaire, just because I am a poet, am pre-eminently representative of human baseness. My state is in no way exceptional, but my awareness of it is itself exceptional. Not for a moment do I lose sight of the fact that my nature, like that of all mankind, is a degraded nature, and that the dirt I tread on covers a place essentially foul and dark, where the whole of creation, owing to a fault committed at its very beginning, one that irremediably flawed the essence of it, lapsed forever from its initial purity.

With Baudelaire self-awareness assumed from the outset a complex character. He was conscious to an extraordinary degree of experiencing in himself a destiny shared by all men, by all beings; and he was conscious of that destiny as being the consequence of a lapse that had occurred at the very source of life.

It was as if at the moment he was created the first man, and with him all his descendants, had suffered an inexplicable mutation, so that thereafter, in all the time it remained for them to dwell on the earth, men were condemned to be drawn willy-nilly in two opposing directions, conscious of enjoying a certain inheritance, of possessing certain natural powers, yet dispossessed of those gifts, deprived of that inheritance.

After a certain time of life Baudelaire coupled this dual, contradictory awareness with a religious belief —belief in original sin. Religion with him, as Marcel Ruff has shown, was a heightened form of Jansenism. For Baudelaire, as for the followers of St Augustine and Jansenius, man's natural depravity is the consequence of an initial lapse entailing the loss of a happy and glorious primary state. In the face of the general disbelief in original sin, which in his eyes was a glaring instance of the blindness of the nineteenth century, Baudelaire took the opposite view. Original sin was only too true. Its influence alone explains the dual nature common to all men, which none, looking inward, can fail to discern in the depths of his being.

This duality is, so to speak, vertical. Theological space is an abyss. The sinner is he who, overborne by the weight of his guilt, is cast down to the bottom of a precipice. There is no other fundamental relation for him but that between the high and the low. It is a matter of falling. For Baudelaire as for Victor Hugo, man is essentially a being marked by the experience of living in the abyss into which he has fallen. But with the author of the *Fleurs du Mal* this descent into the pit has none of the brutality of the fall of the human (or angelic) being in Hugo. In the latter case the fall is at once overwhelming and unending. It is a hideous substitution of emptiness for fullness, a tragic going astray in the immensity of a world superseded by its contrary, nothingness. In Baudelaire, on the other hand, the descent of the damned proceeds at a slower pace. It is never so quick but that it may not be recorded step by step by him who is on the way down. And so the poet can measure at a glance "the dizzy stairs my soul stumbles down"; and if the damned go without light down "eternal stairs with no railing," yet they follow its winding turns step by step.

It goes without saying that the spaces traversed here have not the perpendicular character of vertical space. The damned of Baudelaire follow an inclined plane on which they can be observed at every step of their downward progress. They do not pass without transition from the heights to the depths, from good to evil; they yield, on the contrary, to the invitation of a gentle yet irresistible slope. Stage by stage they go on their destined way.

One of Baudelaire's early poems contains the following passage:

> Il est un puits profond, symbolique Géhenne
> Où trône la Débauche, immonde et sombre reine,
> Un escalier sans fin tourne dans ses parois.
> Le chemin qu'on y fait ne se fait pas deux fois;
> L'amour tombe étouffé dans l'air qui s'en exhale.
> De degrés en degrés au bas de la spirale
> Elle ira descendant, pauvre être dégradé,
> Jusqu'au fond ténébreux que nul œil n'a sondé.

(A deep pit there is, symbolic Gehenna / Where Debauchery reigns, foul and sombre queen, / An endless staircase winds in its walls. / The way once taken is not taken twice; / Love stifles in the air exhaled there. / Step by step to the foot of the winding stair / She will go downward, poor degraded being, / Down to gloomy depths unsounded by any eye.)

No need yet to consider what these gloomy depths may mean (though they are the most important place in the spaces of his mind). Here something more must be said about the downward movement which in its windings leads from one extremity of existence to the other. It brings to mind the movement by which the prisoner in Piranesi's *carceri* is governed. The itinerary followed by the damned of Baudelaire in the dark regions described by the poet traverses a world that is essentially Piranesian. Yet Piranesi is never mentioned in Baudelaire's writings. No matter. There is no need to prove that the poet was directly influenced by the artist. An indirect influence is obvious. Indeed, as Luzius Keller has recently shown, the Piranesian conception of the world left its mark on many French poets of the nineteenth century. Nodier, Hugo, Nerval, Musset, Gautier, all in their own way transposed into verse the peculiarly Piranesian vision of ruins and prisons. Vast halls made to seem even vaster by a series of staircases, along which disappears and reappears a figure, always the same, the prisoner or the damned man, hastening from landing to landing on his way to perdition. To find that obsessive image, Baudelaire had only to read the poems of his elders and contemporaries. What is more, he could not help finding it at the very centre of a book which he particularly admired and would have liked to comment upon and translate on account of the similarities he found in it between the world described there and his own mental world. For De Quincey's *Confessions of an English Opium-Eater* (1822) is in fact nothing but a prodigious rhetorical amplification of the theme of a man obsessed by a single, continually repeated train of thought, a man who, in his obsession, seems to be mounting an endless staircase which cannot lead to deliverance but only to some bitter end. Nothing could be more Baudelairean, well in advance of Baudelaire, than this description of a sufferer held captive not so much by the walls that shut him in as by the steps he takes to escape his fate but which only lead him the more inexorably toward its fulfilment. Piranesi's world and Baudelaire's are alike. Each throws light on the other, so much so that the latter comes to seem like a verbal commentary on the former. It is essentially the world of the abyss, meaning not a place one falls into and dies in, but rather an intermediate region midway between top and bottom, between light and absolute darkness, between hope and despair, a halfway place which symbolizes the impossibility of any positive relation between the two extremes it separates from each other.

It is a purely mental world, a world of dizzied restlessness, which opens up between two parts of the mind between which the lines of communication have been cut.

It is a world which, alternatively, may be described as taking the form of an immense ceiling crowning the dark edifice of the inner man, and which represents the total absence of communication between the place where being starts from and the place it leads to.

"It seemed to him [De Quincey] as if, every night, he descended indefinitely into abysmal spaces without light, beyond any known depth, with no hope of coming up again."

Vain indeed is any hope of coming up to daylight again, for between the light of day and oneself stands a screen which prevents the day from triumphing over the night. Into the place Baudelairean man sinks into, "no eye of Heaven penetrates." Over it, on every side, lies a gigantic lid. That vault is not only a place of unfathomable gloom, "where never

enters roseate and cheerful ray"; it is also and above all the place outside which, out of reach, stands everything roseate and cheerful. The sinking of Baudelairean man into the abyss has then as its consequence the creation over the abyss, up above, of a transcendental sphere—a transcendental sphere whose distant presence, inaccessible and perfectly alien to what it transcends, can only be conceived as the representation of the essential difference between the transcendent and the transcended. Such are "the absent coconut palms of remote Africa" dreamed of by the wild-eyed Negress "behind the immense wall of the fog." Thus the ceiling, the curtain, the lid stand as an opaque, impassable barrier beyond which lies the lost happiness. The thickness of that barrier is such that it constitutes a kind of negative depth, a spatial and temporal distance far too great for the mind to cross it. This distance is the past; not the lost and dreamed-of past lying back beyond original sin, but the past which has elapsed since the original sin, the tainted past. It stretches back into time like the field of an existence irremediably sullied over its full extent. Nothing is more strictly worked out in Baudelaire than this system of a dual past, a remote and radiant past followed by another, a dark, irreparable past.

Baudelaire is the poet of irreparability and remorse:

> Pouvons-nous étouffer le vieux, le long remords,
> Qui vit, s'agite et se tortille,
> Et se nourrit de nous comme le ver des morts?

(Can we stifle the old, the long remorse, / That lives, that stirs and writhes, / And feeds on us as the worm on the dead?)

The past to which this remorse refers is not the happy past directly evoked by nostalgic thoughts. What is remembered here is, on the contrary, the ineradicable succession of lapses by which, in the

course of a lifetime, a man has brought about his own downfall and forfeited the patrimony that was rightfully his. The mnemonic image that stood foremost in Baudelaire's mind, like a haunting spectre never to be conjured away, was that of a blighted beauty, a tarnished happiness: this is what he meant by "flowers of evil"—the bloom of happiness and goodness blackened into its opposite. Baudelaire as he grew older was haunted by his iniquitous past. To him, it was a standing reproach, an ill-omened image of himself which, like a curse, dogged him through life: "I am like a way-worn man whose backward glance, into the deepening years, sees only disillusionment and bitterness."

These *années profondes*, these deepening years, are referred to repeatedly in Baudelaire's writings. They designate many moods, from extreme dejection to extreme delight. But whenever the poet does look back over the gulf of past years (and he does so often), the effect upon him is that of a characteristic intensification of self-awareness. For Baudelaire, a man's life is a vast span of unbroken continuity, a receding vista at every point of which he recognizes the man he was and is. I, Baudelaire, am not simply in the moment in which I am living now; I am a lengthening line which, as it lengthens, does not vanish from the path it has already followed. This is no doubt the reason why Baudelaire seeks, at one and the same time, to recall his past and to escape from it. How could he help recalling it? To live, after all, is to be conscious of time's steady turnover, the transformation of Present into Past. But think of the horror a sensitive man feels at realizing that what is done and past cannot be undone. Baudelaire was acutely conscious of that process of perpetuation by which all

Piranesi (1720-1778). Prisons, plate VII.

that falls into the past comes to rest and stands fast. The poet of remorse, then, is also the poet of an irremediable state of things from which all freedom of action and being has passed away; a state of things that hardens inalterably as it passes from Being to Been. So that now in one form, now in another, now damned and descending the stairs with no handrail, now an icebound ship, but always the toy of fate, Baudelaire sees himself as the hopeless victim of some diabolical Providence which, having decreed an irrevocable destiny for him, takes good care that her decree shall be strictly and relentlessly observed.

Thus time, with Baudelaire, is usually seen as following a predetermined course; its unfolding is contained in its prior history. Neither present nor future can ever belie the *decree* of the past. Time is no longer a becoming; it is a state that persists. "There are such things as everlasting situations," wrote Baudelaire, "and everything connected with the irremediable falls into this category." Everlasting situations are those in which future and present are indistinguishable from the past that shapes them. There is accordingly a Baudelairean way of looking at things in which the depth of existence is simply the unfolding, as far as the eye can see, of a single human landscape: a landscape reflecting the same monotonous characteristics, a time-trap in which all men are ensnared.

It was doubtless this sense of being trapped that made Baudelaire, in a letter of 1861 to his mother, speak of the "continuity of horror" that he saw stretching out before him. Faced with the same prospect a few years before, when placed under the care of a guardian who hedged him round with restrictions and obligations, Baudelaire was infuriated, to such a pitch that he suffered fits of vomiting and dizziness: "I saw before me," he wrote, "a never-ending succession of years with no family, no friends, no girl friend..."

The irreparable, then, was the never-ending. It meant the reduction of time to a sinister eternity, like the everlasting detention and deprivation reserved for the punishment of the damned. The latter, in the absolute uniformity of their existence, have but one preoccupation: remembering their unalterable past. Such is remorse. It becomes the sole object of one's thoughts; the mind fixes on it to the exclusion of all else.

Time, with Baudelaire, means permanence, but of a special and particularly malefic sort: destructive permanence. "The irreparable gnaws with its accursed tooth our soul, sorry monument." In one sense, time appears unmoving, almost unchangeable. In another, it is seen as never for an instant ceasing to annihilate everything contained in it. The essential operation suggested by the action of gnawing is that of an imperceptible but incessant destruction of being. As Baudelaire put it: "Time eats away life." Then he immediately added that this obscure enemy "gnaws the heart." "Man," he says elsewhere, "is blind, deaf, brittle as a wall shaken and gnawed by an insect." And again: "Time engulfs me minute by minute, as the snow's immensity a stiffened body."

Time then is at once small as an insect and vast as space. On the one hand it is reduced to a minute but incessant corrosion. On the other it swells till it fills all space, on a scale where time ceases to exist because movement has ceased to exist. This ultimate disappearance of time, merging with the permanence of space, fired Baudelaire's imagination. He described it in the form of a gradual slackening:

> *Je jalouse le sort des plus vils animaux*
> *Qui peuvent se plonger dans un sommeil stupide,*
> *Tant l'écheveau du temps lentement se dévide.*

(I envy the lot of the lowliest animals / Who can sink down into a dull sleep, / As the skein of time slowly unwinds.)

The motionlessness of time thus produces the same effect as the unification of space. In the result, both induce an intense feeling of boredom. The ennui of Baudelaire resembles in some ways a tormenting deprivation of being, which is the ennui of Pascal. It also recalls the lethargy that was apt to come over the eighteenth-century man of feeling. But it is at the same time something quite positive: the persistence of a state which has become unbearable because of its invariability. Further, it is an awareness of that invariability, in other words of the irrevocable character of fate. So that on the one hand Baudelairean man recognizes with ever-increasing intensity the immutability of his lot, while on the other he strives to dismiss from his mind all thoughts of it; hence his desire to take refuge in endless sleep. The boredom described by Baudelaire is thus a complex form of experience. It is a maximum of awareness with a minimum of action; or more exactly it is a maximum of awareness which has both as its cause and its consequence a minimum of action. Hence the length of time perceived in that intensification of awareness and in the absence of any other activity:

Rien n'égale en longueur les boiteuses journées
Quand sous les lourds flocons des neigeuses années
L'ennui, fruit de la morne incuriosité,
Prend les proportions de l'immortalité.

(Nothing compares in length with the limping days / When under the heavy flakes of the snowy years / One's boredom, fruit of bleak incuriosity, / Assumes the proportions of immortality.)

The prodigiously heightened consciousness of time results in a sense not only of indefinite extension but of oppressive heaviness. Time is a crippling load to bear. Though it may quicken the power of thought, it paralyses the creative powers. After Vigny, Lamartine and Nerval, and before Mallarmé, Baudelaire is one of the French poets who suffered most cruelly from sterility. "I felt myself attacked by a disease like that of Gérard [de Nerval], namely the fear of being unable to think any more or write another line." "The fear," as he described it, "of seeing the admirable poetic faculty, the clearness of thought, and the power of hope which really constitute my capital, of seeing all that waste away and disappear in this horrible existence full of commotion."

Very early in his working life Baudelaire experienced this impotence, "terrible and impassable as the icy wastes of the pole." The dread of its return never left him, and indeed always tended to increase the likelihood of its return. This dread augmented in almost monstrous proportions the dualism of the poet's spiritual life: on the one hand an intense self-awareness, on the other an equally intense awareness that that self was nothing, no more than an absence of being.

This accounts for the need Baudelaire felt to impose a sort of unity upon himself by suppressing one of the antagonistic tendencies at work within him.

That effort of suppression he described as "the vile and repulsive but sincere wish" to sleep on forever: "There are times when the desire comes over me to sleep and sleep without end." — "Let me sleep! Sleep rather than live." — "Submit, O my heart; sleep the sleep of the brute."

This submissiveness, in effect an abdication, led him to brood over suicide. One day when thinking of taking his life, he wrote a long and very fine letter. The gist of it is that he is killing himself because he can no longer face life, because "the weariness of going to sleep and the weariness of waking are unendurable."

Only an unbroken sleep seemed bearable to him. But sleep is never quite unbroken. Dreams arise which betray our innermost longings. As Jean-Paul Sartre has aptly pointed out, Baudelaire was perpetually goaded by the desire to be somewhere else, away from his inertia, away from his remorse, away from the consciousness of his degradation. To long to be elsewhere is, at the same time, to long to be someone else, to have a different self, a different nature, in a different place. So Baudelaire's obsession with travel implies much more than the merely geographical aspect. What at heart he longed for was an eschatological change. This will appear more clearly later, when we come to examine the means whereby Baudelaire tried to escape from his fundamental predicament—the state of a fallen being. The dream of happiness that wafts him to an imaginary India or Holland transfers him ideally to a place where he is allowed to revert to what he was, or become what he should have been, before his lapse, in the state of what theologians call pure nature. Nevertheless, without laying any undue emphasis on these travels to an allegorical country, it should be noted that Baudelaire's journeys, his mental journeys that is, have in fact no destination and no end: "But the real travellers are those alone who leave for leaving's sake." Where they are going they do not know. And if in the end they choose to go to their death, they choose it because it is not a positive destination. It is not a definite or discoverable *place*. It is simply *yonder*, somewhere as different as possible from the detested *here*: "The first inn on the way" or "The place where you are not."

In a word, the essentially wandering character of Baudelaire's thought is such that it has no final purpose or ideal in view. His thought never tends to conform (as Lamartine's does, for example) to a model which either preceded it in the form of some age-old idea or anticipated it in the form of some end to be achieved. Nothing could be less Platonic than Baudelaire's thought. It does not project before it, into the future, some definite type of beauty and happiness which it hopes in due course to encompass and comply with. Indeed, what is even more serious, it has the greatest difficulty in giving the future any positive shape at all. Setting aside a small number of recurring dreams (to be dealt with in the next chapter), we must admit that Baudelaire proved incapable of picturing any distinct future. For him, the future meant simply the chance of throwing off the crushing burden of the present and escaping at a bound from the temporal conditions of existence. In his mind, the Elsewhere and the Future had above all a centrifugal function: they were a pure *beyond* devoid of any characteristics.

> Viens! oh! viens voyager dans les rêves,
> Au delà du possible, au delà du connu!

(Come, oh come and travel in dreams, / Beyond the possible, beyond the known!)

It is clear that in these lines (and many such could be cited) the movement of the mind neither joins the cosmic movement nor does it rise to a point from which it might better embrace it. In no sense can Baudelaire be considered a poet of the cosmos. He is neither a Dante nor a Milton, still less a Lamartine. In Lamartine, the movement of the verse tends to accompany things in their movement of ascension or flight. The movement of Baudelaire's verse is the flight of the mind *away* from things and, at the same time, away from the place where, amidst those things, the mind runs the risk of being forever tied down. In a word, by that very movement, one of horror in the presence of his real being, Baudelaire hastens to put as much distance as he can between himself and himself. It is only by taking his distance that he can put up with himself.

One of the main Baudelairean themes is that in which an object is seen at the greatest possible distance, in the depths of space or time, on the farthest verge of the horizon. Such is the case with the sunsets he describes. Their purpose is to project into the gulf of distance not only the light of day but everything it illuminates, not only tangible objects but mental objects that haunt the mind. The setting of the sun is thus tantamount to the setting of human consciousness, the sinking of consciousness into a twilight zone of somnolent reverie where thought is drained of all content:

Vois se pencher les défuntes années
Sur les balcons du ciel, en robes surannées;
Surgir du fond des eaux le Regret souriant;
Le soleil moribond s'endormir sous une arche,
Et, comme un long linceul traînant à l'Orient,
Entends, ma chère, entends la douce Nuit qui marche.

(See the departed years lean out / From the balconies of heaven, in faded robes; / Smiling Regret arise from the watery deeps; / The dying Sun fall asleep beneath an arch, / And, like a long shroud dragging in the East, / Hearken, dearest, hearken to sweet Night's oncoming tread.)

Here it is as if one were watching the remote take shape before one's eyes—the remote or, what amounts to the same thing, the past. It is true that the Baudelairean past tends to remain in the mind in the form of an ever-present past, an image close at hand and accordingly one of intense actuality. Is it not possible however to throw back the past to the farthest point on the horizon? Then the pain and bitterness of it will lose its sting. What Baudelaire is trying to do in the above description of a sunset is to *sweep away* into the farthest distance the past and the whole procession of memories that accompany it: together they recede in solemn order and go down with the sun, so that (as Baudelaire elsewhere writes) the sunset becomes "the marvellous allegory of a soul full of life, that *goes down behind the horizon* with a magnificent provision of thoughts and dreams."

The beauty of this image lies in the fact that what seems to dip behind the horizon is not just a fragment of life but a whole existence. To the depth of the perspective corresponds the length of the procession traversing it. But this is not all. This spiritual plenitude, this totality of being, is on the move. Like a ship under way with its load of passengers, it is bound for a place so far away that the eye cannot follow it long. The dominant impression then is no longer that of a present past which continues to make its weight and bitterness felt. On the contrary, the past evoked here is saddening only because it is moving away. Thus for Baudelaire memories may be painful in two ways: either because they persist in remaining cruelly present or, conversely, because they are felt to be receding sadly into the limbo of past time.

Hence the *plaintiveness* of this latter experience. While remorse is always accompanied in Baudelaire by bitterness ("the long river of gall of previous griefs"), the contemplation of the past across increasing distance inspires in him a serener sadness and milder accents. Even so, the sight of "all that crowd, remote, absent, almost defunct," conjures up a profoundly disturbing image of the poet himself, for it is the image of his own life in its steady movement deathwards. So Baudelaire's contemplation of himself from a distance, across the gulf of years, is rather like taking leave of a person one will see no more. Such a leave-taking is implied in the famous lines:

Comme vous êtes loin, paradis parfumé!...
L'innocent paradis, plein de plaisirs furtifs,
Est-il déjà plus loin que l'Inde et que la Chine?

(How far away you are, fragrant paradise! / The innocent paradise full of furtive pleasures, / Is it already remoter than India and China?)

With plaintive cries, with a kind of modulated sob, the poet tries to recall the faraway paradise and bring it to life in a voice that can only be described as silver-toned. Yet the Paradise evoked is *already remoter* than the remotest lands of the East. The poet measures the distance separating him from it; in his eyes it is an all but absolute distance. Baudelaire is in the habit of casting these long backward glances. He is the wayfarer who halts at sundown and proceeds to reckon up not so much the progress made as the span of life already covered and therefore lost.

This is the case of Hippolyta in *Femmes damnées*:

> *Elle cherchait, d'un œil troublé par la tempête,*
> *De sa naïveté le ciel déjà lointain,*
> *Ainsi qu'un voyageur qui retourne la tête*
> *Vers les horizons bleus dépassés le matin.*

(She tried to find, with an eye baffled by the storm, / Of her artless days the already distant sky, / Like a traveller who turns his head / Toward the blue horizons he passed in the morning.)

This traveller looking back is an image that occurs again and again in Baudelaire. In *La Fanfarlo* Samuel Cramer describes the disillusionment that separates him from the past. "We are all of us rather like a traveller who has made his way across a vast country and who each evening watches the sun, which before had cast a beautiful glow on the amenities of the road, set on a flat horizon." The result of contemplating the past is to make one realize how dull one's present life is, and how inaccessible, beyond recall, one's past life is. All direct experience moreover, by its very intensity, tends to open a gulf between the present and the past. So it is with Hippolyta after the shock of her first experience of Lesbianism. So it is too with the opium-eater, whose memory is both quickened and blurred by the stimulant that has clouded his brain. "He is the traveller who looks back at evening toward the countryside he passed through in the morning, and remembers fondly and sadly the thousand fancies that thronged his brain while crossing those regions now turned to misty horizons."

Baudelaire's experience of depth therefore comes close to merging with that of the abyss. What he evokes is soon misted over and blurred. So far from manifesting itself each time in the form of a relief against anguish and dejection, depth, with Baudelaire, and particularly the depths of memory, often reveals itself as a powerful ferment of despair. In a quatrain of *Le Balcon* depth appears as an inner void:

> *Ces serments, ces parfums, ces baisers infinis,*
> *Renaîtront-ils d'un gouffre interdit à nos sondes,*
> *Comme montent au ciel les soleils rajeunis*
> *Après s'être lavés au fond des mers profondes?*

(Will those vows, those perfumes, those numberless kisses / Be born again from an abyss we are forbidden to sound, / As rejuvenated suns rise into the sky / After being washed at the bottom of deep seas?)

The answer to this, sadly enough, is no. Unlike cosmic phenomena with their inexhaustible power of renewal, the phenomena of the human psyche do not find in their depths the resources necessary to restore their vigor once it has been drained away. The experience of depth, in Baudelaire the most important of all experiences, is with him the experience of a force which, far from restoring, only devours. It is tantamount to the wasting away of being in a vast and sombre region where all forms of life, ideas, emotions, memories, feelings, ultimately sink.

Nothing haunts Baudelaire more than the thought of this yawning inner chasm. He describes it by a name which he thought of giving to his great collection of poems: he calls it "limbo." Speaking of Delacroix's *Women of Algiers*, a painting which profoundly impressed him because of the affinities he saw in it with his own spiritual state, it reeks, he said, of "the vile haunts that lead us soon enough, *into the unfathomed limbo of dejection.*" Delacroix's picture is probably one of the immediate sources of Baudelaire's *Delphine et Hippolyte*, a poem which presents sapphic love as an occasion for the woman who practises it to discover the abyss of her own mind:

> ...*Je sens s'élargir dans mon être*
> *Un abîme béant; cet abîme est mon cœur!*...
> *Brûlant comme un volcan, profond comme le vide.*

(Opening up in my being I feel / A yawning abyss; that abyss is my heart! / Burning like a volcano, deep as the void.)

Helped by Delacroix, who opened "deep avenues for the most travel-minded imagination," Baudelaire thus discovered, not perhaps (as Sartre thinks) the nothingness to which all consciousness comes down in the end, but more precisely the "depth of perspective" which is there revealed whenever consciousness sees it swallow up the elements of the inner life which have begun to furnish it out and give it countenance. Depth is not mere vacuity; it is rather an inner spaciousness, the place of all the mind's activities. This spaciousness is usually revealed in the objects to which the mind directs its thought, but sometimes too in thought itself, in the absence of any object— like the host who, having offered a banquet to many guests, finds himself alone in the banquet hall when they have departed. Connected with the theme of inner depth, therefore, is the theme of the mind's *survival* once all the forms that temporarily occupied it have fallen away. This theme Baudelaire may have owed to Poe, who repeatedly describes the mind's continuing activities in the solitude of the tomb. This is the theme of the living dead, very frequent too in Baudelaire:

> *Dites-moi s'il est encor quelque torture*
> *Pour ce vieux corps sans âme et mort parmi les morts!*

(Tell me if there is any torture left / For this old body soulless and dead among the dead.)

The anguish expressed here does not spring from the knowledge that after death the body is destined to endure fresh tortures. It springs from the fear that that posthumous torture may be accompanied by the consciousness of suffering. Likewise, evoking a figurine by Eugène Christophe representing a woman hiding her tears behind a mask, Baudelaire asks, "But why is she weeping?" and himself gives the answer:

> *Elle pleure, insensé, parce qu'elle a vécu!*
> *Et parce qu'elle vit! Mais ce qu'elle déplore*
> *Surtout, ce qui la fait frémir jusqu'aux genoux,*
> *C'est que demain, hélas! il faudra vivre encore!*
> *Demain, après-demain et toujours! — comme nous!*

(She weeps, you fool, because she has lived! / And because she lives! But what she laments / Above all, what makes her tremble to the knees, / Is that tomorrow, alas, she must go on living! / Tomorrow, the day after and always! — like us!)

The cause of the lamentations described here has nothing to do with the objective character of existence itself. The masked figure weeps because the least bearable of all situations is that in which life goes on indefinitely without being distracted from itself, so to speak, by the events, of whatever nature, that occupy the mind.

In short, at the end of its itinerary, having made what it could of the experience of a lifetime, Baudelaire's thought may be defined in two ways at once similar and contradictory: now as pure depth without objects, now as pure activity of the mind, unreasoning and aimless. Who am I? Baudelaire asked himself. Am I the void I see opening up within me, or am I the movement that crosses it? Am I to recognize myself in the tragic absence of being which confronts me, or in the act by which I confront that absence?

Such is undoubtedly the furthest point reached by a movement of thought doubling back upon itself. Now grappling with the objects of thought, now running away from them, Baudelaire's mind finds itself ultimately in the presence of a depth to which nothing gives life but thought itself—a sort of perpetual motion functioning in the void. So that in one sense Baudelaire's thought tends to lose itself in this vacancy, while in another it can no longer be perceived, in its own mirror, as anything but an unending train of thinking for thinking's sake:

> *Tête-à-tête sombre et limpide*
> *Qu'un cœur devenu son miroir.*

(Dim and limpid tête-à-tête / When a heart is mirrored in itself.)

BAUDELAIRE AND THE WORLD OF IMAGINATION

WHO am I?" Baudelaire asks himself. Or rather, "Who am I not?" In his case, self-knowledge is less the knowledge of the person one actually is than that of the person one is no longer and from whom one is infinitely distant through debasement and debauchery. Baudelaire studies his image in the looking-glass. Whom does he see there, if indeed he still sees anything at all? Never was Narcissus less ready to condone the image of his inferiority, his dissimilarity. The act of conscience becomes a feeling of hate or, worse still, of ironical scorn:

> *Je suis la plaie et le couteau,*
> *Je suis le soufflet et la joue,*
> *Je suis les membres et la roue,*
> *Et la victime et le bourreau.*

(I am the wound and the knife, / I am the buffet and the cheek, / I am the limbs and the wheel, / And the victim and the torturer.)

The point of arrival is a split personality. On the one hand is the torturer; on the other, the tortured. One's thought takes revenge on itself for the shame it feels at being what it is. But one may also assume a different attitude: it consists not in rejecting one's

With regard to original sin, and form molded on the idea, I have often thought that noxious and repulsive animals were perhaps only the vivification and materialization of man's evil thoughts.

Francisco Goya (1746-1828).
"All will fall!" (Todos Cacran!), 1797. Etching.

140

141

shame, in hurling it violently in the face of the person one no longer wants to be, but on the contrary in accepting that shame as the common fate of all those who suffer. Baudelaire often wants only to insult and forswear himself because he realizes his debasement. But there are times when, because of this awareness, he sees himself as the true representative of a debased humanity—debased because robbed of the happiness and dignity it might have enjoyed. To see oneself in this guise is also to see oneself double. It is to see oneself as one is and to dream of oneself as one might have been. When this happens one's dominant feeling is not self-hate but melancholy. "When an exquisite poem," he writes, "brings the tears to our eyes, these tears are not a proof of excessive pleasure, but rather a token of an irritated melancholy, of a postulation of the nerves, of a nature exiled in imperfection that only wants to enter, here and now, a paradise that has been revealed to it."

Thus melancholy is a complex state of mind: it is the awareness of an unattainable perfection and of of a too obviously attained imperfection. "Mingled pain and pleasure," as Baudelaire says. And in this simultaneous contemplation of two worlds that exclude each other, the poet might end up by draining the last of his resources, did he not possess a certain number of remedies for the melancholy to which he is a prey. These remedies he clutches all the more desperately because—in contradiction to what has been said so often—he is not one of those who give up the fight at the first blow. Baudelaire, the poet of the irretrievable, is also and, as it were, at the same time the man who says: "Everything can be retrieved." For him hope is not only the contrary of despair, it is the other aspect of the same affective situation. To pass from one of these two feelings to the other it is sometimes only necessary to reverse one in order to reveal the other. "One must achieve a creation by the logic of contraries," he himself once wrote. As he said in another context, "To blasphemy I shall oppose heavenward yearnings; to obscenity, Platonic flowers." If we are to grasp the value of this statement, we must realize that in Baudelaire's eyes the heavenward yearning is a result of the blasphemy and that veritable Platonic flowers bloom only in the midst of obscenity. Hence the debasement of the personality is not beyond repair; the remedy derives paradoxically from the very movement by which the debasement is consummated. Just as there is a counter-religion (namely, an upside-down religion), there is a movement of recovery through which the counter-religion turns itself, so to say, right side up. If I believe in the devil, I already believe in God. This is the religion—first practised in the wrong way and later turned round the right way—that Baudelaire puts in practice in *Les Fleurs du Mal.* "To extract beauty from evil," to use his own words, is to transfer beauty from evil to good. A life-saving exercise *in extremis*, an act not of folly but of reason pushed back to its last line of defenses. The conviction that realities which are poles apart attract each other and end up by coinciding.

So we must not be surprised if the remedy Baudelaire craves for is so often formulated in the same terms, even when he addresses his prayer to apparently incompatible beings. An example of this is the admirable couplet:

J'implore ta pitié, Toi, l'unique que j'aime,
Du fond du gouffre obscur où mon cœur est tombé.

(I implore pity from Thee, the only one I love, / From the bottom of the dark pit in which my heart has fallen.)

To whom is this couplet addressed? To a benevolent or a malevolent being? In like manner, the following line,

Soyez béni, mon Dieu qui donnez la souffrance,

(Blessed be Thou, my God who givest pain,)

does not differ at all in tone and sentiment from this one:

O Satan, prends pitié de ma longue misère.

(O Satan, take pity on my long misery.)

If, as Baudelaire says, prayer is a "reservoir of force," that force may be directed, almost indifferently, in one direction or the other. Black magic and white magic are the same. Baudelaire makes no distinction between them: "In prayer there is a magic operation," he says. It is that alone which counts and not the being to whom the prayer is addressed—God or Satan, the principle of good or the principle of evil. Thus in Baudelaire we repeatedly find an awareness of a supernatural presence, whose beneficent action, by suspending the course of fate, confers on its beneficiary a way of feeling and thinking, a "state of mind," which is totally different from that imposed upon him by his debased nature. Hence there is no doubt that this intervention, which Baudelaire prayed for repeatedly all his life, plays a part in that life similar to the part played by grace in the Christian theology.

It would be wrong, however, to confuse these two graces altogether. Christian grace is essentially redeeming. It aims at endowing man with the means to save his soul. The grace implored by (and sometimes granted to) Baudelaire is of a totally different kind. It tends to restore man to what the theologians call the state of pure nature, that is to say, "the state of man before the Fall." The magical power of grace purifies the person on whom it acts from his taints and so makes him look and feel like an angel: "I prefer to consider this abnormal state of mind," says Baudelaire, "as a veritable grace, a magic mirror in which man is invited to see himself in beauty, namely as he should and could be: a sort of angelic exaltation."

The important point for Baudelaire is that this state must seem to be absolutely gratuitous, that is to say, not determined by any previous state. This enables him, at least provisionally, to evade the concatenation of events that constitute his destiny. "A marvellous state in which a man's spirit finds itself as if by a special grace." So, in contrast to everyday life and the state of mind that life produces, there is a diametrically opposite state in which, all of a sudden with no transition or apparent reason, genius blossoms out in grace and bliss. The very gratuitousness of what one feels becomes the guarantee of its authenticity. Whether happy hazard, divine caprice, stroke of luck, or the reversal of everlasting bad luck, the fact of experiencing happiness is proof, somehow, that happiness actually exists. Consequently, the first way in which Baudelaire makes his dream come true is by remaining open and available in order to derive the greatest possible advantage from the "visitation" that comes to inspire him.

He might no doubt have been satisfied with that result and remained in expectation of fortuitous happenings which could not only change his life but whose occurrence would adorn certain favored hours. But he did not have it in him to be satisfied with merely temporary changes. It was not enough for him to feel momentarily redeemed: his life had to be transformed to the very end. A life that is entirely corrupt, tainted to its utmost depths, can only be *ransomed* by a grace that purges it through and through. Baudelaire yearned passionately not only, like Banville, for a cluster of "happy hours," but for a life that would be constantly happy, a permanent state of bliss. One of his most typical traits was the "dream of eternity," which aimed at replacing time and its tragic persistence with a diametrically opposite state in which his whole life would be spent in a permanent heavenly bliss. Since he could not rest content with the rare, intermittent visitations of grace, he had perforce to seek out other ways to attain the eternity on earth for which he longed.

In his *Notes nouvelles sur Edgar Poe* he wrote: "Poe made great efforts to subject the fleeting demon of the happy minutes to his will." Like Poe, Baudelaire was far less the poet of grace than the poet of human effort. Not, perhaps, of the effort actually exerted, the will power actually brought to bear, but of the effort *dreamt of*, the will power viewed as an instrument of magic transformation.

> *Architecte de mes féeries,*
> *Je faisais, à ma volonté,*
> *Sous un tunnel de pierreries*
> *Passer un océan dompté.*

(As the architect of my enchantments, / By my will I forced / A tamed ocean to pass / Through a tunnel of precious stones.)

"We have regenerated our soul," said Baudelaire, "by alternate work and contemplation; *by the assiduous exercise of our will power* and the permanent nobility of our intention, we have created for our own use a garden of true beauty." Work, concentration, the daily exercise of will power, enable one to replace the being one actually is with an idealized version of oneself. Just as there is a "gymnastics suitable for strengthening the will," there are means suitable for giving one's dreams the tangibility of the things perceived by the senses. In other words, there are methodical procedures for remedying the imperfection of reality. One of them is mnemotechny. Baudelaire, as we have seen, was obsessed by all sorts of unhappy memories. But he was also haunted by happy memories—memories of lost happiness recalled one day by the sound of a bell or the scent of a flower; memories of happiness that a woman's loosened tresses or the caresses and odors of her body conjure up in our mind's eye as in a vast inner space of blissful shores, blue skies and distant oases. All this teeming life of memory is not, in this case, a fortuitous grace: it is the product of an art, the result of an act of will.

> *Je sais l'art d'évoquer les minutes heureuses*
> *Et revis mon passé blotti dans tes genoux.*

(I know the art of conjuring up the blissful minutes / And relive my life nestling between your knees.)

And if the scent of the loved one's hair uncorks a host of memories, that too is due to an explicit act of will. "I *want* to wave it in the air like a handkerchief," says the lover. Hence poetry and the poetic state that is at once its cause and its effect are no longer fruits of chance. By a deliberate act of thought, the poet's spirit can place itself, as if for ever, in the most fruitful hours of his life. They alone are worth preserving and reliving. Art is an evocative magic, a mnemotechny of the beautiful. This is most clearly visible in painting, and particularly in that of Eugène Delacroix which, as Baudelaire said, "derives chiefly from memory [and] addresses itself chiefly to memory." Or again, "I sometimes see Delacroix's work as a sort of mnemotechny of man's inborn grandeur and passion."

No less mnemotechnical, in Baudelaire's eyes, was the new painting by Boudin, Manet and a few others he discovered towards the end of his life. For, in contrast to what many people believe, the recording of direct impressions was not Impressionism's only task; it also used reminders of all sorts to render at a given time the impressions the artist had previously received. "If (the spectators) had seen, as I recently saw at Monsieur Boudin's... several hundred pastel studies improvised before sea and sky, they would understand... the difference between a study and a picture... Boudin knows very well that all this can only become a picture *through the poetic impression recalled at will*."

Here we have the essential statement. Painting, poetry and all other forms of art are solely means to recall at will certain feelings and states of mind. Genius itself, no matter what its sort, "is but childhood *regained at will*," in other words a supple, tractable mnemonic power that can be used by the person who possesses it to conjure up in his mind's eye, and therefore in the work he produces, a certain number of experiences that were stored away during his childhood. For a poet it is more or less the same as for a painter. In fact, Edgar Allan Poe, like Delacroix, subjects to his will "the fleeting demon of the happy minutes" and states that "he alone is a poet who is *master of his memory.*"

It is clear to see that, though they have some points in common and though Proust himself referred to Baudelaire as to a precursor, the latter's mnemotechny differs enormously from the method used by Proust. In fact, if for Proust as for Baudelaire remembrance is the recovery of childhood's impressions, in Proust's eyes there was no hope of recovering those impressions *at will*. What is more, Proust only asked of memory to help him recover a timeless essence. Baudelaire demanded something more than mnemonic experience. What he wanted was the abolition of his state as a debased creature and his installation once and for all in a changeless bliss. For him mnemotechny was a means to "interfere with his destiny and replace it with a new kind of fate," a happy fate whose peculiar role would be to replace the disastrous destiny of the debased being.

Consequently, Baudelaire's cult of childhood must be understood in this very precise perspective. A child is not an angel. Still quite close to original sin, it is a barbarous being, as dangerous as it is nasty. But it has one essential gift, the gift of childish perception, which no adult can rediscover and usurp. "A child sees everything as if new; it is always inebriated. For it no aspect of life has lost its shine."

In short, there is in a child's vision of the world "a compulsive idealization which is the result of a... sharp perception that innocence renders magical."

In certain conditions an adult may experience the same "enthusiasm of mind and senses" either by recovering powers he formerly possessed or by drawing belatedly on the innocence he has stored up. "There are days when a man wakes up with a young, vigorous genius; hardly have his eyelids rid themselves of the sleep that sealed them than the outer world appears to him in high relief, clear outlines and a wealth of colors that are quite miraculous." In this extremely important passage magical keenness of vision is made manifest in two different ways—by the clarity of the outlines and the wealth of the colors. The outlines are sharply defined, the colors penetrate the brain "with a victorious intensity." In a word, "the senses are more perceptive and record sensations that are more intense." What is more, the intensity of sensation is matched by the originality of the imagination. The invention of the imaginary is superimposed on the perception of reality. A magical transformation of the natural world and the spectator's inner nature is thus achieved.

All Baudelaire's thinking can be reduced, as we have seen, to the opposition between (debased) nature and a state (dreamt of) which would be above it. Imagination is the means to overcome this opposition. Of a sudden nature coincides with the dream world. Of a sudden the being one is, freed from its physical and moral ugliness, begins to resemble the being one has dreamt of being. This double transformation is not due to mere chance, to a divine or devilish grace, but to an act performed by the subject himself who, by using his imagination, extracts heaven from hell and a flower of beauty from the evil in which he is forced to live.

The most magical aspect of imaginative activity is therefore the supernatural interest with which it clothes an external and internal universe that till then was condemned to proffer the most dismal appearance. "A magical varnish *that spreads over all life ...colors it* with solemnity and *illuminates its depths."* By illuminating the depths of life, the varnish of the imagination once more gives Baudelaire's vision of life the additional dimension and inner spaciousness, that we have already recognized in an earlier chapter. But what a change has been achieved by the magic of the imagination! For one who is aware of our universal perversion, nature is a narrow vault closed by a ceiling and it is only beyond this ceiling that open space exists. But through an act of the imagination the universe opens up and becomes a "deep immensity" through which the mind gaily ploughs.

What is most elating in Baudelaire is the dream in which he sees himself flying, swimming, sailing in a vast expanse. His greatest dreams are dreams of expansion. Dreams in which, the better to match the infinite power of dilatation enjoyed by human thought, the expanse deepens leaving thought free to move about; dreams in which thought seems to expand or, better still, to seize itself in the very act of taking possession of space. Taking possession of supernaturalized nature occurs as a definitely quantitative process, an ecstatic proliferation. By analogy with the act of creation, begetting the universe in the shape of a "numberless population of numbers," the poet achieves awareness of the multitude of peculiar, distinct entities that make up the universe. Thus the perception of what is tends to turn into something like a huge "arithmetical operation in which numbers beget numbers," as occurs in certain musical performances listened to under the influence of hashish. Baudelaire is perhaps the only French poet who possesses in the highest degree the intuition of the numerical dynamism that is always manifest in the slightest movement. "Number is a translation of space," said Baudelaire; it is a numbered space that grows indefinitely by reason of the movement that takes place in it. Number inflates space and tends to make it burst.

However, the multiplying movement with which we are concerned here cannot be properly perceived by a stationary spectator. It is only by accompanying the mobile on its trajectory that thought can encompass the full amplitude of the movement. This is the way we often witness in Baudelaire the rising tide, whether real or metaphorical:

D'où vous vient, disiez-vous, cette tristesse étrange,
Montant comme la mer sur le roc noir et nu.
Et du haut du divan elle souriait d'aise
A mon amour profond et doux comme la mer,
Qui vers elle montait comme vers sa falaise.

(Whence comes, you said, this strange sadness, / Which rises like the sea over the bare, black rock. / And enthroned on the divan she smiled with pleasure / At my love deep and gentle as the sea, / Which rose towards her as towards its cliff.)

In this assimilation of the mounting tide of feeling to the mounting tide of the sea we can distinguish a vast collective yearning which is on the point of developing into an ample wave-motion.

For Baudelaire there are also privileged places, where we can see the origin of a motion that later develops in space. For instance, the seaports, where ships set sail "for a far-off sky." Here too the poet stresses the cinematic analogy between a woman's body and the sea and the objects that float upon its surface:

Quand tu vas balayant l'air de ta jupe large,
Tu fais l'effet d'un beau vaisseau qui prend le large,
Chargée de toile, et va roulant
Suivant un rythme doux, et paresseux et lent.

(When you walk sweeping the air with your wide skirt, / You are like a fine ship that puts out to sea, / Under full sail, and rolls along / With a rhythm that is gentle and sluggish and slow.)

A peculiar feature of the magic of motion in Baudelaire is that it coincides exactly with the verbal image invented by the poet and so offers the reader a stylistic version that fits it perfectly. It is as if physical space and the space occupied by the words are identical, and the dynamic rhythm of the poem develops in this new space with the same ease as a ship at sea or a woman taking a walk. The slowest possible motion is one of those that Baudelaire reproduces best. But it would be wrong to confuse this sluggish slowness with the tragic slackening, the gradual stoppage of all effort of which I spoke in the previous chapter. Here the subject does not tend towards total immobility, which is a metaphorical form of annihilation. Whenever movement seems to be on the point of ceasing, it starts up again with the same smoothness but in a different direction. Such is the rocking motion that is always linked in Baudelaire's mind with the idea of rhythm and gentleness:

> Et mon esprit subtil que le roulis caresse
> Saura vous retrouver, ô féconde paresse,
> Infinis bercements du loisir embaumé!

(And my subtle spirit which the roll caresses / Will find you again, O fruitful sloth, / Infinite rockings of fragrant leisure!)

"The bliss of being rocked, which Baudelaire has sung in words one cannot forget," says Jean-Pierre Richard, "depends on its tranquillity, its harmony, its profound accord with the person who receives it. The see-saw motion balances and swings life round a fixed pivot." Hence in Baudelaire's rocking motion there is duality and complexity. The fixity of the pivot is both matched and contrasted by the see-saw action. And the latter gives the idea, not of a single movement, but of a succession of movements that obey the same generating principle. This pinpoints the great importance of *rhythm* in Baudelaire's poetry. In fact, rhythm is essentially a regular plurality of movements that harmonize in their succession. In other words, rhythm is first of all an *undulatory* phenomenon: "Who among us has never dreamt of a peculiar, poetic prose in which to render the lyrical movements of the spirit, the undulations of reverie and the convulsions of consciousness?"

The manifestation of this undulatory lyricism demands a quantity of elements seized in a movement that co-ordinates them. Thus Baudelaire compares the movements of a woman's body in the clothes and ornaments she wears with "an undulating, sparkling, scented apparatus." This expression stresses the immense multiplicity of womanhood and its gait at once *smooth* and *rhythmical*. In Baudelaire's phrases and imagery there is not merely a single rhythm; there is a combination of rhythms in harmony. That is what he calls "eurhythmy."

The term denotes a motion at once *simple* and *multiple*, *constant* and *varied*. A collective reality, be it a woman, a frigate or a complex sentiment, moves in one's mind or in the space around one as a synthesis of connected elements that balance each other. Like a structure made up of various components that can be isolated but are doubly linked by a certain natural affinity and a certain similarity of movement. Few images delighted Baudelaire's imagination more than these forms, at once plural and mobile, in which the eye glides from one aspect to another, from one viewpoint to another, watching them change incessantly but without ever failing to obey a principle of order that conditions them and preserves their cohesion in movement. Thus the clouds in the sky, no less than the dreams of the spirit, appear to Baudelaire in the typical aspect of a *mobile architecture*: "Through the open window of the dining-room I contemplated the *moving* architectures God makes with vapors—vapors, those wondrous structures of the impalpable."

Perhaps this peculiar mobility, which is joined here with the normally static appearance of architectural forms, is best observed in seaports, places subject more than any others to the changing action of light and water: "A port," says Baudelaire, "is a charming abode for a soul exhausted by life's struggles. The broad sky, the *mobile architecture* of the clouds, the changing colors of the sea, the twinkling of the beacons, are a prism wondrously suited to amuse the eyes without ever tiring them." We rediscover Baudelaire's preference for ports in the taste he shows for the female body, for it too is a mobile architecture: "He loved a beautiful body," said Baudelaire of his prototype Samuel Cramer, "like a material harmony, like a *beautiful architecture plus movement.*"

Architecture plus movement! Order in diversity and diversity in order! Baudelaire's thought takes pleasure in these harmonious contraries, and above all in Delacroix's pictures. What do we find there? The same thing as in nature's spectacles, that is, says Baudelaire, an infinite series of lines, curved, twisting, broken, "in obedience to an unerring law of generation, in which parallelism is always vague and sinuous, in which concavities and convexities match and pursue each other."

The sinuous lines of Delacroix's pictures, like the lines in nature, form a mobile architecture. An architecture that appears at first glance to be concealed by the profusion of viewpoints and the multiplicity of forms. The fact is that these latter constitute, in relation to the fixity of the central motif, a variety of successive aspects that is essentially temporal. So much so that it is not too far-fetched to pretend that any picture by Delacroix develops both in space and in time. Thus time extends and enriches space. This is particularly obvious in a natural phenomenon which, more than any other, caught Baudelaire's attention—the phenomenon of light. Who does not know the magnificent passage at the beginning of the third chapter of his *Salon of 1846*? It is truly a paean in praise of color: "Let us imagine a beautiful natural space in which everything is verdant, everything glows, glistens, sparkles in absolute liberty, where all things, diversely colored in accordance with their molecular structure, *changed from one second to the next by shifts of light and shade...*"

Time, as Baudelaire sees it in the generative movement that produces a multitude of different aspects, is truly an enrichment of space. Thanks to the almost imperceptible changes that take place in time, space develops, becoming more complex and more apt to show up the many qualities it possesses. Once again we find ourselves in the presence of what we may well call Baudelaire's mathematical genius, his capacity of capturing reality in all its multiple aspects. Here, however, it is not a question of perceiving a simple numerical reality. In his perception of space and time in the innumerable relationships they form, Baudelaire reveals what we may call a geometrical genius alongside his arithmetical genius. It occurs in his *Fusées* and deals, once again, with a ship and might refer to a woman walking: "I think that the infinite, mysterious charm one finds in the contemplation of a ship, particularly a ship in motion, derives in the first case from the regularity and symmetry that are one of the human spirit's primordial needs, no less than complication and harmony; and, in the second case, from the *successive multiplication and generation of all the curves and imaginary figures* produced in space by the real elements of the object."

Thus Baudelaire does more than merely explore the depths of space; he also discovers the "complications" that spread their branches there. This second discovery involves something so fascinating and reveals such riches that Baudelaire is often tempted to focus his attention exclusively on this aspect alone. He sees it if not as the most magical, at least as the most abundant and the most numerous of them all, the one that most directly captures an artist's imagination. That imagination, as he said of Constantin Guys, is "as if assaulted by a host of details, each of which demands justice, with the fury of a crowd enamored of absolute equality."

This abundance may be compared with the prolific development of a teeming vegetation. Baudelaire loves to yield to the ecstatic vertigo produced by the "arabesque of sounds" and the "sinuosity of lines." He passionately enjoys the "many-hued, variegated beauty that moves in the infinite spirals of life." "It is," he says, "an immense pleasure to make one's home in the seething, the undulating, the moving, the transient and the infinite." Nonetheless, in Baudelaire awareness of motion is not merely awareness of the host of co-ordinates that motion generates in every single point of its trajectory. The complication of reality is neither irrational nor anarchic. It is governed by a principle that is no less important than the capacity for variation and proliferation.

Baudelaire was led to consider motion in the same dualistic perspective as all his other experiences. Motion is *dual*. It is both a rectilinear impulse towards a goal and the sum total of all the traceries that meander round the path of that rigid impulse. This does not mean that Baudelaire admits the supremacy of the straight line. For instance, his hero Cramer "had a profound loathing—and in my opinion he was perfectly right—for long straight lines where apartments were concerned and for architecture imported into the home." In exactly the same way Baudelaire loathed the drawings of Ingres and his disciples because he suspected them of subjecting curves to straight lines. On the other hand, he praised Delacroix for not allowing his originality to be encroached upon by the system of straight lines: "His figures are always restless and his draperies in a flutter."

Yet neither Delacroix's painting nor Baudelaire's poetry accept the supremacy of mere teeming abundance. They are governed simultaneously by two principles—the principle of rectilinearity and the principle of imaginative exuberance—which tend to join forces.

Under the influence of De Quincey, Baudelaire imagined the marriage of the straight line and the curve in the symbolic shape of a thyrsus or a caduceus. Let me recall the prose poem he dedicated to that capricious emblem. "What is a thyrsus? …a staff …Round about this staff stems and flowers disport themselves in capricious meanders, the former sinuous and crooked, the latter drooping like bells or overturned cups. And an amazing glory springs from this *complexity of lines*. Does it not look as if the curved line and the spiral court the straight line and dance around it in silent adoration?"

In the preceding passage Baudelaire has merely followed, though with evident pleasure, De Quincey's image, adding a few touches here and there. But he goes on to a development that is a very precise expression of his own way of thinking. A way of thinking once again dualistic, in which the opposition of the straight line and the curve becomes the opposition of intellectual rigor and imaginative fancy: "The thyrsus is the representation of your amazing duality… The staff is your will, straight, firm, immovable; the flowers are the twisting path your fancy traces round about your will, the feminine element that performs its prestigious pirouettes around the male. Straight line and arabesque, intention and expression, stiffness of the will, suppleness of the word, unity of the goal, variety of the means, all-powerful, indivisible amalgam of genius, what artist dares to divide and separate you?"

...beasts of the night,
Whose wide-staring phosphoric eyes make
The night's shadows loom yet more opage.

William Blake (1757-1827).
Hecate, about 1795. Engraving.
Tate Gallery, London.

150

What artist is capable of seizing in its complexity what is at once the duality of creative thought and the duality of the object that thought grasps? The thyrsus is at once will and caprice, but it is also unity and multiplicity. As we have already seen, Baudelaire's universe appears in the dual aspect of depth and complexity. Sometimes, as in the case of the thyrsus, the poet represents this dual aspect in the shape of a first movement, simple and direct, that leads towards the depth of the spirit, while at the same time a second movement embraces space with all the ramifications of its co-ordinates. Sometimes this dual aspect of space is revealed by another form of the association of contraries, by the harmony and contrast displayed, in so many representations of space, by the multiplication of lines in the foreground and the simplicity of the background. We must examine this if we are to understand how Baudelaire's imagination supernaturalizes space by gaining control over it.

There is, in fact, in Baudelaire's work a motion that has often been described. It is the movement of a mobile object that travels in front of a stationary background. This motion is expressed in various ways. Strange fanfares pass by under a murky sky; the rising tide spreads over a bare, black rock. Hearses pass through the streets of a city, the image of a splenetic soul. Monuments stand out before a deep space. Thus psychedelic visions spread their colors, their thrills, their lights on life, whose depths they reveal.

No matter what metaphorical or real motion the poet suggests, the motionless background against which the mobile object stands out is nearly always represented in the shape of a dark expanse. In the poem *Le Chat*, a voice "rises and shimmers *over my darkest depths.*" In another poem, entitled *Confession*, remembrance springs *"from the dark depths of my soul."* On the one hand we find the surge or current of the thought that flows through the spirit; on the other we find the spirit itself, described as a dark depth that contrasts with the mobile luminosity of intellectual life.

Thus for Baudelaire the affirmation of movement, life and light frequently tends to join with and lean against a contrary, negative reality—the absence of movement, life and light, which forms its background:

> *Je suis comme un peintre qu'un Dieu moqueur*
> *Condamne à peindre, hélas! sur les ténèbres.*

(I am like a painter whom a mocking God / Condemns to paint, alas! on darkness.)

If a poet is a painter who paints on a background dark as night, the same is true of a musician. Poe moves his phosphorescent figures against purplish, greenish backgrounds. Wagner, in his ardent, tyrannical music, "paints on a background of darkness, torn by reverie, the vertiginous conceptions of opium." Lastly, speaking of himself, Baudelaire says:

> *Sur le fond de mes nuits, Dieu de son doigt savant*
> *Dessine un cauchemar multiforme et sans trêve.*

(On the depth of my nights, with his deft finger God / Draws a multiform nightmare that gives no respite.)

Hence, in the life of the mind there are two distinct elements, two different levels. There is on the one hand a first state of mind, like a dark space, whose monotony nothing breaks; on the other there is the procession of images. As a rule those two levels are superimposed; sometimes they intermingle. Thus in Baudelaire a curious reversal of the usual relationship of night and light is expressed in the theme of Twilight, which he treated many times. On the one hand, twilight is the agony of the light, its slow engulfment in a "vast, black nothingness." The day is destroyed by "the victorious oppression of the night." An oppression that not only brings about the gradual extinction of vanquished light, but also the stoppage of its correlative—movement. When the night covers the sun with its veil, it drowns it "in its congealing blood." All that is left, sole vestige of daytime animation, is the eddying scent of the flowers and the last sounds of diurnal life. We get the impression of a slow slipping of life into nothingness, of light into night, of the present into the past. But the struggle between night and day does not end quite so definitively as one might believe in the victory of the death principle. "Through the black present pierces the delicious past," the "luminous past" whose "last vestige is harbored" by the heart. Thus the all-devouring night becomes the means by which the images thought saw sink or disappear are restored to it. Twice this resurgence of the past in the shape of memory is represented as a new emergence of light in the midst of shade: memory *"shines* like a monstrance"; the stars *"light up* . . . under the night's deep mourning." In one of his prose poems Baudelaire uses a marvellous metaphor to describe this reappearance of the light through the dark veil that covers it: "It is like one of those strange costumes worn by dancers in which a dark, transparent gauze lets us glimpse the muted splendors of a gorgeous skirt. . ."

Hence twilight is not simply the setting for the triumph of night over day. It marks a positive relationship between initially hostile elements. Instead of seeing, as in the previous passages, a nocturnal background against which luminous figures stand out, here we have a curtain of shadow pierced by points of light. Whether it moves against a background of darkness or pierces it with points of fire, light never ceases to be associated with the thing that veils it; it forms with its opposite a complicated relationship that is hard to unravel.

Let us now consider the non-solar nature of certain lights that are diffused in the night and seem to spring from the night. Any light that does not emanate directly from the sun seems more beautiful to Baudelaire and more meaningful for the very fact that its source is a different principle from that of daylight. It has often been observed that Baudelaire's world is rather nocturnal than diurnal; it is a world lighted by oil lamps and gas lamps; in which even a candle has an important part to play owing precisely to the fact that the weak light it casts is enclosed in a vast circle of darkness: "Nothing is deeper, more mysterious, more fertile, more gloomy, more dazzling than a window lighted by a candle."

In Baudelaire's world the rays of a candle are often linked with the darkest night. They touch and clash, and each gains in dramatic power through their mutual relationship. As in the combinations of chiaroscuro we see in some painters of the Mannerist school, in Rembrandt and in Delacroix, Baudelaire's imagination finds its greatest satisfaction when the contact between the two hostile elements is so close that they exchange their contrasting properties and each tends to turn into the other. When light becomes darkness and darkness light.

Let us take a look at the picture of the naked woman in the poem *Les Bijoux:*

> Et la lampe s'étant résignée à mourir,
> Comme le foyer seul illuminait la chambre,
> Chaque fois qu'il poussait un flamboyant soupir,
> Il inondait de sang cette peau couleur d'ambre.

(And when the lamp had resigned itself to die, / Since the hearth alone lighted up the room, / Each time it fetched a flaming sigh, / It drenched that amber-hued flesh with blood.)

At first sight, what seems to count most in this scene is the general dimming of the light. As in the theme of twilight, the gradual decline of the sources of light consummates the triumph of the powers of night. Yet what remains is the impression of a transfer. The light continues to shine, not without weakening but still with a certain persistence, shifting its focal point from one object to another, from the lamp to the hearth and from the hearth to the body on which it projects its glow. Gradually, as his phenomenon takes place, the quality of the light seems to change so that what it loses in intensity it gains in intimacy, in warmth, in truly human life. As if its reddening glow was the sign of a basic alteration in the quality of the fire, almost warranting the belief that, at a distance, the embers are transformed into a flower of flesh and blood. This confirms the idea that in Baudelaire's eyes light is never endowed with such magic power as when it is totally different from *natural* light. I mean, the light of the sun. This is true no doubt, in a certain sense, of all artificial light. Artificial light, whatever its source, always seems to the person it illuminates to be *distinct from* daylight. But in Baudelaire this distinction assumes the appearance of an illicit substitution. The moon, a lamp, the hearth, a woman's flesh, are stars whose ever briefer rays usurp the functions of the sun. Like Prometheus, they steal its fire. If charming twilight is the friend of crime, if it comes like an accomplice with stealthy steps, that is because it too commits a crime. Furtively, it replaces the lawful light with a stolen light, a light that unlawfully becomes an independent source.

We can see this happen in *Les Bijoux*. Secretly, when every other source of light has been, or is on the point of being, extinguished, when the lamp has resigned itself to die and the hearth fetches its last flaming sighs, then the woman's flesh, drenched with a reddish glow, becomes in turn a source of light. Thus, though Baudelaire does not say so explicitly, that flesh seems, through the successive substitution of one source for another, to have finally become the centre from which the light is diffused. It assumes an independent luminous power, alchemistically formed by the metamorphosis of the fiery force of the hearth into blood and of blood into luminous flesh.

We are now in a better position to see what Baudelaire's poetry tends to achieve. What he wants is to replace, whenever possible, the single light of day with a number of independent lights. And in this way to replace in his own personal universe, the simplicity of heavenly light with an indefinite number of sources of light. Baudelaire's world is a world of lamps, of chandeliers, of lanterns, of lighting fixtures of all sorts, whose task is to intercept, modify, recreate and retransmit light.

Woman's flesh and woman's jewels are the most brilliant of these fixtures. Nothing, indeed, is more typical of Baudelaire than the woman-mirror or the woman-reflection which sparkles or glitters with an infinity of lights of which she is, if not the original source, at least the centre they presently spread from.

This radiance of the female body, either of itself or through its adventitious ornaments, is never so bright as when it is linked with its direct opposite, the obscure nature of masculine thought. To dream of a woman is to illuminate one's own darkness. When this beneficent light casts its beam upon one condemned to live in darkness it may flood his soul with peace and joy:

> *Mon âme par toi guérie,*
> *Par toi, lumière et couleur!*
> *Explosion de chaleur*
> *Dans ma noire Sibérie!*

(My soul healed by you, / By you, color and light! / Explosion of heat / In my dark Siberia.)

There is a very evident dichotomy in a passage of this sort. It is like one of those contrasts of black and white that occur so frequently in Petrarchian or Baroque poetry. But Baudelaire's poetry tends rather to suggest a dubious complicity between light and night. Its ideal would be a substance at once luminous and obscure, source of light and principle of darkness. In the feminine world we find this in the shape of black hair, which is dark by definition but doubly luminous because when it hangs loose it displays its lustre and because its suggestive power conjures up an image drenched with light. It is on the one hand a "sea of ebony," on the other the origin of a "dazzling" dream. In Baudelaire verbal synthesis links delightfully these contrasting features:

> *Cheveux bleus, pavillon de ténèbres tendues,*
> *Vous me rendez l'azur du ciel immense et rond.*

(Blue hair, pavilion spread with darkness, / You give me back the blue of the vast, round sky.)

The optic of memory turns the perspective of the sky upside down, like a cloudscape reflected in a lake. Here, instead of enfolding from above and without the world over which it spreads its azure dome and on which it pours its light, the sky is entirely enclosed in a tent of dark hair, confined in a pavilion of darkness. The magic spell cast by a woman's loosened hair transforms the blue of the sky into the centre of an inner world whose walls are the night.

Of course one finds other sources of inner light in Baudelaire, excitants are unquestionably one of them. For those who use them, excitants create a centre of inner light. Thus wine provides the drunkard with visions that are "illuminated by the inner sun." In Baudelaire's words sensual pleasure lights "a flame in our underground vault."

In short, for Baudelaire any deep-seated or intense movement in the world of the imagination tends to appear as a luminous current that emanates from the most obscure depths of the spirit and yet illuminates it. It is this inner current which Baudelaire admired so greatly in *Madame Bovary*, terming it "a sickly faculty, subterranean and rebellious, that passes through the entire work, ...*an obscure vein that illuminates*—what the English call a *subcurrent*— and acts as a guide through the pandemoniac chaos of solitude."

Let us imagine a source of light that is at once a lamp, a jewel, a vault, a river, in which the substantial obscurity of thought combines with its opposite, the brightness of dreams. This theme is rendered most completely in the underground river of *Rêve parisien*:

> *Et tout, même la couleur noire,*
> *Semblait fourbi, clair, irisé;*
> *Le liquide enchâssait sa gloire*
> *Dans le rayon cristallisé.*

(And all, even the color black, / Seemed polished, bright, iridescent; / The liquid enshrined its glory / In the crystallized ray.)

Here we have a luminosity that is at once bright and dark, subterranean and sunlit, moving yet congealed in crystal. Here the union of opposites attains its highest point. Moreover, nowhere else is the independence of local color so clearly stated. The poet is the creator of an architecture of luminous enchantments based on a principle of exclusively inner lighting. In other words, he annexes light and makes it his own prerogative. To do so he must perforce imprison light in the narrowest possible compass, for instance in a room with the windows covered by curtains or shutters:

> *Je fermerai partout portières et volets*
> *Pour bâtir dans la nuit mes féeriques palais.*

(Everywhere I shall close curtains and shutters / To build my fairy palaces in the night.)

To build a truly fairy palace, the "architect of his enchantments" first had to close the place to be illuminated in order to prevent the light of day from competing with the light of night. So that night becomes the authentic creator of light. On a par with the night is the gaze of the loved one which, like the black sun of Victor Hugo, Gérard de Nerval and the occultists, is at once dark and bright. "Her eyes are two caves in which mystery sparkles vaguely, and her gaze lights up like a flash of lightning: it is an explosion in the dark. I would compare it with a black sun that pours out light and bliss."

Delicious fruit of the night, flower of evil or misfortune, "black yet luminous," this nocturnal light expresses a fundamental paradox of Baudelaire's universe. In its complex nature it unites the two incompatible principles of good and evil, beauty and ugliness, light and dark. Baudelaire may render this "simultaneous double postulation" simply in the shape of an absolute contradiction. But sometimes he makes an effort to surpass that contradiction in order to attain an imaginary vision in which irreconcilables are reconciled and contradictions are smoothed out. When this happens, it is no longer a question of presenting a real world in which good exists in evil, beauty in ugliness, and light in darkness, but a suprareal or infrareal world in which good is evil, beauty is ugliness, light is darkness. Must I remind you that this world is the world of the Gnostics and occultists in which, owing to the reassessment of all values, good is found in the heart of evil, beauty in the heart of ugliness, and darkness is the only light? Not merely a light in the night, a light issuing from the night, but a light that is black, a light that is fundamentally dark. This is the extreme concept of light sometimes formulated by Baudelaire.

We find it in a line of *Les Ténèbres*: "It is She, black yet luminous," and again in this passage in the essay entitled *L'Œuvre et la vie de Delacroix:* "It seems to you that a magic atmosphere has advanced towards you and envelopes you. Sombre yet delicious, luminous yet tranquil, this impression... has its place for ever in your memory..." We find it in *Rêve parisien*, where everything, even the color black, seems polished, bright and iridescent. We find it in *L'Irrémédiable*, the poem in which the poet faces up to himself, in which the phosphorescent eyes of viscid monsters "make the night darker still," symbolizing thought's encounter with itself:

> *Tête-à-tête sombre et limpide,*
> *Qu'un cœur devenu son miroir!*
> *Puits de Vérité, clair et noir,*
> *Où tremble une étoile livide...*

(Dim and limpid tête-à-tête / When a heart is mirrored in itself! / Well of Truth, clear and black, / In which trembles a livid star...)

As in the dim staircase of *Igitur*, where polished panels that form mirrors reflect to infinity the image of the person who descends, Baudelaire's thought thrusts down into this confrontation, this identification of light and shade, to reach a zone where night is no longer merely the creator of light but light is the creator of night.

BAUDELAIRE AND HIS KINDRED SPIRITS

IN the prose poem entitled *Les Yeux des Pauvres*, Baudelaire describes a dream whose realization would be no less essential to his happiness than the union of his mind with nature or that of light with darkness. What he dreamed of was the union of his own mind with that of other people. Speaking of himself and his mistress in a prose poem, he wrote: "We promised each other that we would have all our thoughts in common and that henceforth our two souls would be one." In this poem, the attempt at a "marriage of true minds" is doomed to failure. Far from mirroring each other's thoughts, the two minds assert their differences. And the poet concludes that "thought is incommunicable, even between those who love each other."

Baudelaire is thus forced to recognize man's fundamental solitude. To be born is to burst asunder some indefinable bond of union, to be flung headlong into a world where, between people, even between mother and son, mutual understanding is impossible. In 1839 Baudelaire wrote to his mother: "And when I feel within me something that uplifts me, it might be a violent desire to embrace everything, or simply a beautiful sunset at the window, *to whom can I say it?*" To whom, meaning if not to you? If only he could confide his innermost feelings at once to his mother, how reassuring and soothing it would be. But the way he puts the question betrays a strain of anxiety. Even were one's mother present, it would be difficult, perhaps impossible, to communicate what one felt. It may be that even in her son's presence a mother is always absent, and the same is true of our friends, our mistresses and all those who inspire us with a desire to be with them and in that nearness to forget that we are alone.

Man's solitude is universal. It is, like all the rest, a consequence of the original sin. It is part and parcel of that general fatality which prevents us from living in harmony with fallen nature and its denizens. Every break in that solitude is illusory.

What then is to be done? Resign oneself to endless solitude? Or, what is worse, consent to have with other people relations which can only be either ambiguous or hostile? Baudelaire was often tempted to accept the latter alternative. In his relations with others he relied for his defense on either irony or hatred.

"The man with a mind of his own, who will never agree with anyone, should lay himself out to enliven the conversation of fools and the reading of bad books. He will derive a bitter relish from it." Such was his irony.

Now for his hatred: "I may as well blurt it out. Sheer pride keeps me going, and a savage hatred of all men. Always I hope to be able to dominate, to have my revenge..."

By turns ironic and aggressive, Baudelaire's misanthropy was unrelenting and all-embracing.

It applied to everybody. It found on all sides good reasons for resentment and scorn. Everywhere and always, it seemed to him, man offers "the tedious spectacle of everlasting sinfulness." Here was the basis of the ignoble equality of all human beings. All are flawed, all incur the same blame. Extending to God himself the sense of this solidarity or similarity in evil (a view already held by Joseph de Maistre), Baudelaire saw all men as strangers who yet were intimately bound together by a terrible equivalence.

It was the idea of this equivalence which made the poet say to his mistress: So long as your dreams have not mirrored Hell, so long as you have not felt the embrace of irresistible disgust, you have no right to tell me, "I am your equal."

So there is an equality in shame, as there is too perhaps in crime: "We are all hanged or deserve hanging." But if that is so, here is an unexpected means of getting in touch with each other. All men are our fellow creatures. In spite of the law of incommunicability which affects us all in equal measure, the similarity of our natures and the analogy of our behavior offer us a last chance of comparing our lives and, consequently, of understanding each other.

At the very beginning of the *Fleurs du Mal*, Baudelaire salutes the reader in blunt and peremptory terms: "Hypocritical reader, my fellow man, my brother!"

Here, needless to say, he is not being whimsical: his words are meant to be taken seriously and literally. Just because he *is* the poet's brother and fellow man, and in spite of their common hypocrisy, the reader will readily understand what is being said to him. The poet appeals to the confraternity in evil of all those who like himself feel themselves to be at once culprits and victims. All men are made alike. Each one, in his heart of hearts, knows what the plight of others is: it is the same as his own. In another poem Baudelaire again turns directly to the reader, in terms that amplify his original invocation:

> Mais si, sans se laisser charmer,
> Ton œil sait plonger dans les gouffres,
> Lis-moi pour apprendre à m'aimer.

(But if, without falling under the spell, / Your eye can plunge into the abyss, / Read me and so learn to love me.)

And he added a warning to the reader:

> Plains-moi! sinon je te maudis.

(Pity me! or else I curse thee.)

The hypocritical reader is thus called on to pity and even to love the writer in whom he will discover the same penchant for the abyss as in himself. He and the writer he reads are two speleologists, two explorers of the depths. They recognize each other as having had the same experiences. Perhaps this feeling will enable them to take a liking to each other. So there is a chance of overcoming the obstacle of solitude and arriving at some degree of mutual sympathy and understanding. Baudelaire dreamed of enjoying the balm of womanly comforters: guardian angels, Muses, or Madonnas. He imagined them warming his heart, guiding his steps. One name was often on his lips, that of Electra —the criminal's sister, who soothes his gory dreams and mops the sweat from his brow. She is made one with her brother by the compassion aroused in her by the knowledge of the murky depths through which the murderer's thoughts wander. Between beings so sadly solitary as men, there springs up a kind of intelligence based on the crimes they have committed and the ills they have suffered. The first way in which it becomes possible to surmount the universal incommunicability is through the complicity of pity.

So it is in a moving passage of the *Journaux Intimes* in which, overcome by the thought of their life together as it really is, wholly compounded of misbehavior and disputes, Baudelaire and his mistress mingle their tears. "A tremor went through her; she too felt herself moved to tears and stirred." Here, in the mutual comprehension of the "deepening years," something very different from hostility or irony emerges; something which, in the midst of discord, restores harmony to sundered hearts.

Baudelaire felt a constantly recurring need to join in the daily life of other people, to "espouse the crowd." Nothing could form a sharper contrast with the sense of incommunicability which he felt at other times. "The poet," he wrote, "then enjoys this incomparable privilege, that he can at will be himself and others. Like those wandering souls in search of a body, he enters as he pleases into the character of each man."

True, this looks on the face of it like the expression of a very different feeling from the previous example. To identify oneself with the crowd, is that not to surrender to a purely gregarious yearning? May it not be described as a need for "fraternitary prostitution," to use an expression coined by Baudelaire himself?

Even so, the desire to immerse oneself in the crowd must not be confused with the desire to identify oneself with the multitude which makes up that crowd. The pleasure of mingling with the crowd, writes Baudelaire, is "a mysterious expression of the enjoyment of the multiplication of numbers." The poet, the dandy, the painter, the sketcher, out to catch an expression or a gesture, are drawn to the crowd because they find in it an inexhaustible source of human material. Far from embracing with eye or mind an undifferentiated mass, they record *in detail* with amazing rapidity all the individual traits which, one after another, arouse their interest.

"The lover of universal life enters the crowd as he would an immense reservoir of electricity. He may be likened to a mirror as vast as that crowd; to a kaleidoscope endowed with consciousness, which, at each of its movements, represents the manysided life and the moving grace of all the elements of life."

In a word, to experience the crowd in its ever-changing multiplicity is to experience the human number. Assembled humanity presents itself to the eye. But it is not perceived as a totality; it is merely a composite multiplicity, each of whose elements taken singly attracts the eye. So there is no essential difference between the way Baudelaire's thought "espouses the crowd" and the way he espouses individual beings. No, the really important thing here is the knack Baudelaire has (in common with writers and artists like Bruegel, Balzac, Delacroix, Constantin Guys) of becoming passionately interested in those who happen to be the object of his attention. Then the barrier of incommunicability is broken down. At one bound, by a movement which first seizes the physical features and then infers the moral characteristics, Baudelaire's eye and mind penetrate to the secret places of the heart.

The most striking example of this insight is the poem of the "little old women," *Les Petites Vieilles*. "In the devious recesses of vast capitals," the poet's eye is caught by the old women, "disjointed monsters," who live there. They have for him "a bizarre and captivating attraction." Out of curiosity he observes their gestures, their ways, the wrinkles of their wizened faces. He sees through them, he divines their whole past and private life:

> *Sombres ou lumineux, je vis vos jours perdus!*
> *Mon cœur multiplié jouit de tous vos vices!*
> *Mon âme resplendit de toutes vos vertus!*

(Whether dark or bright, I live your vanished days! / My manifold heart delights in all your vices! / My soul glows with all your virtues!)

The vices and virtues which these wretched crones had practised in the faraway days of their youth, and which now—not for them but in the imagination of an observer—become again a source of pleasure and glowing pride. That observer identifies himself with these withered old women. Inwardly he lives over all that they have felt and experienced. And indeed this identification is so complete that it implies the resurrection in him of all the vices and virtues practised by them in the past.

Contrary to what some critics have assumed, Baudelaire shows in this instance, and others as well, that he is the reverse of an egoist, if by this term we mean a person who is wholly wrapped up in himself. Unlike the genuine egoists who are constitutionally unable to take more than a condescending, momentary and purely surface interest in others (George Sand, for example), he found within himself a generous enough fund of sympathy, of fellow-feeling, to project himself into other people's lives and live them over in their historical depth.

So it would be quite wrong to write off Baudelaire's power of identification as no more than that of an actor. Admittedly, as he said himself of his alter ego Samuel Cramer, he happened to be endowed with an "acting faculty." But the actor must also be a historian. A portraitist does not only paint a face or figure; he paints a whole life stretching back over a span of time. Insight into others goes far beyond appearances. It is a matter of entering into the life of an individual, of sharing it, of following its course through the years in the genesis and development of its destiny.

But how is such a thing possible? How, by what methods, is a man to transcend the state of absolute solitude and arrive at this searching insight into the private life of others?

The answer to this question is of great importance. On it depends in the last resort the significance to be attached to Baudelaire's critical and aesthetic thought, and in particular to his notion of harmony and analogy.

An initial harmony, in the Baudelairean sense of the term, is that which exists between the different parts of an object. Harmony in this sense appears as an interrelation of the elements of which the object is composed. Take a picture by Delacroix. It is perceived in its harmony when the different means of expression employed by the painter seem to operate in such a way as to reveal their analogy to the spectator. Between the color and the drawing, and even more than that, between the particular tones of the coloring and the varied and sinuous strokes of the linework, an indefinable identity reveals itself. To perceive a picture by Delacroix is to replace an analytical scrutiny of its elements by a synthetic vision. Such a vision is possible only if the spectator's eye passes from the perception of the parts to the perception of the whole. In each of the parts, the eye *recognizes* a resemblance to all the others. But for this act of recognition there could be no overall comprehension of the picture.

In the same way, for Baudelaire a woman's beauty is perceptible in the overall effect of harmony, present in each and every aspect of her person. Each particular detail acts in concert with all the others to make one *recognize* her unique type of beauty:

> *Et l'harmonie est trop exquise*
> *Qui gouverne tout son beau corps*
> *Pour que l'impuissante analyse*
> *En note les nombreux accords.*

(And the harmony is too exquisite / That governs all her lovely body / For impotent analysis / To note its numerous accords.)

Woman then is a perpetual metaphor. Each of her attractions re-echoes all the others. Synesthesia is the means by which all the charms she is mistress

Woman is above all a general harmony, not only in her bearing and the movement of her limbs, but also in the muslins, the gauzes, the vast and shimmering clouds of fabrics in which she drapes herself.

Edouard Manet (1832-1883).
Lola de Valence (detail), 1861-1862.
Louvre, Paris.

of are transformed into fresh charms. She appears as a synthesis of distinct elements which become identified with each other. Now this transposition can only be effected in the mind of an onlooker. The woman is a picture which, if it is to take on its full value, must undergo in the spectator's mind what Baudelaire calls a "mystical metamorphosis." The act of looking is concomitantly an act of imagination and memory; to look is to summon up one's whole stock of recollections and to find within oneself a series of equivalents of the object one is looking at. This is true even for the most disconcerting objects, even for mean and ugly ones. If I admire a picture by Goya, it is first of all because the contortions and grimaces of the fiendish creatures I see in it bring home to me "the analogy and harmony that exists objectively in all the parts of these beings"; but it is also, secondarily, because all these beings, in spite of their bestial faces, "are imbued with humanity." Although they are hideous, or perhaps just because they are hideous, they disclose a similarity to the person who is looking at them. He finds himself taking a personal interest in them.

In a thousand ways, then, the universal analogy materializes. In a thousand ways objective reality is transposed into a mental image. This every woman knows who, by finery and make-up, by a "sublime distortion of nature," becomes in the eyes of her admirers "magical and supernatural."

The same is true of nature taken as a whole, degraded and fallen no doubt, but always ready to "assume a supernatural interest." Thus the painting of Delacroix and the writings of Edgar Allan Poe are "translations" which introduce the supernatural into objective reality.

This supernaturalizing of nature is nowhere more conspicuous in Baudelaire than in his description of cities. It is enough to stroll through the streets for mystery and enchantment to arise at every step:

Fourmillante cité, cité pleine de rêves,
Où le spectre en plein jour raccroche le passant!
Les mystères partout coulent comme des sèves
Dans les canaux étroits du colosse puissant.

(Teeming city, city full of dreams, / Where the ghost in broad daylight accosts the passer-by! / Mysteries everywhere flow like sap / In the narrow channels of the mighty colossus.)

There is in Baudelaire a fantastic realism which has its source, as he himself confessed, in the landscapes of the romantic painters. He liked nothing better than "great lakes that represent immobility in despair, immense mountains, stairways from the planet to the sky, fortified castles, crenellated abbeys, gigantic bridges, Ninevite buildings wherein dizziness dwells..." It was this supernaturalism that prevented Baudelaire from caring much (apart from Corot and Théodore Rousseau) for the landscape painters of the French school. He found them, as he put it, "overly herbivorous animals." Baudelaire did not like "irregular plant life." What he did like, however, were stones and stony landscapes. Hence his preference for the painters and engravers who invented fantastic cities.

We have already said that there is no mention of Piranesi in Baudelaire's writings. Yet what he evokes in his description of opium dreams is very much a Piranesian vision: "Astonishing and monstrous pieces of architecture arose in his brain... Dreams of terraces, towers, ramparts, rising to unknown heights and plunging to immense depths."

This is a Piranesian dream if ever there was one, though inspired not directly by the plates of the Italian etcher but by the reading of De Quincey, who had already so marvellously transposed the fantastic world of Piranesi into his prose, which Baudelaire translated into French.

There seems to be still another source for Baudelaire's vision of fantastic cities. It is to be found in a passage that occurs both in his *Salon of 1859* and in his study of Théophile Gautier. There is, writes Baudelaire, a painter, a "musing architect," whose name he is not quite sure of (the painter he meant was the English artist H. E. Kendall), who "builds up on paper cities whose bridges have elephants for piers, with gigantic three-masters in full sail passing between their legs."

But if, directly or indirectly, the fantastic townscapes of Baudelaire's imagining seem indeed to be of Piranesian origin, there was another great artist, this one a contemporary of his, in whom he found the exact equivalent of his own supernaturalism. Meryon's scenes of Paris have nothing of the inordinate fantasy and violently dramatic character of Piranesi's etchings. But they do have an equal power of suggestion and the same capacity for transforming reality into a genuinely poetic image.

Of Meryon, Baudelaire wrote: "I have rarely seen the natural solemnity of an immense city represented with more poetry. The majesty of accumulated stones, the spires pointing to the sky, the obelisks of industry vomiting against the firmament their coalitions of smoke, the prodigious scaffolding of monuments undergoing repairs, bringing to bear on the solid body of the architecture their own openwork architecture of so paradoxical a beauty, the stormy sky charged with anger and malice, *the depth of the vistas increased by the thought of all the dramas contained in them*, none of the *complex* elements composing the sorrowful and glorious setting of civilization was forgotten."

One can readily understand why Baudelaire found Meryon's etchings so much to his liking, for they combined the "complexity" of the elements with the "depth of the vistas."

And depth and complexity, as we have already noted more than once, are the essential features of Baudelaire's poetry, just as they are of Meryon's art.

Depths rendered complex by the thought of all the dramas contained in those immense vistas.

For a city does not consist of architecture alone, of houses and buildings: it consists also in the people who live in them. Baudelaire, eager student that he was of the manifold individualities to be met with in city crowds, admired the painters and draughtsmen capable of recording these fleeting faces and scenes —artists like Hogarth, Charlet, Gavarni, Constantin Guys, above all Daumier, the Goya of city life:

"Dip into his work, and you will see passing before your eyes, in its fantastic and arresting reality, everything a great city contains in the way of living monstrosities. Nothing in its wealth of all that is frightening, grotesque, sinister and farcical but Daumier is familiar with it."

Thus by a phenomenon which moreover is ceaselessly repeated, Baudelaire, in front of a picture he admires, is not content with an outward appreciation of the forms and colors. To the fantastic world of the picture his own world corresponds. A whole world of "frightening wealth" is also hoarded up in Baudelaire's mind. The grimacing figures that people the painter's pictures and the images that obsess the poet reveal their sameness.

The poet then is not only a poet. He is one in whom there arises a complex of images analogous to the vision of others. It is a matter of insight, or second sight, an act by which Baudelaire, in his capacity as critic, is able to reflect the works which appeal to him.

That Baudelaire was a great critic, the greatest of his time, there can be no doubt; but it may not be clear why he was so great a critic. The reason is that his critical activity in no way differed from his activity as a poet. Baudelaire was the only critic of that day who, in his criticism as in his poetry, constantly made use of his imagination. With him, these two great literary forms were one. His poetry is a critical poetry; his criticism is a poetic criticism.

This is evident in the process of identification by which Baudelaire recreates or rediscovers within himself the equivalent of the book he has read or the scene he has been looking at. One thinks again of the poem of *Les Petites Vieilles*, the sight of those poor crones, the intentness with which the poet gave his whole mind to them, the intuition which enabled him to relive their lives, to remember their past as if it were his own. Is it not exactly the same thing that occurs when Baudelaire *experiences* the painting of Delacroix? That painting, like the poetry of Baudelaire himself, is essentially suggestive. His are the pictures which "recall to memory the greatest number of poetic thoughts and feelings which, though once experienced, one supposed were buried forever in the night of the past."

To the creative mnemonics of the painter correspond then the memory and the recreative imagination of the critic. Speaking this time not of Delacroix but of another artist, Constantin Guys, Baudelaire wrote: "Faithfully translating his own impressions, [Guys] emphasizes with instinctive energy the salient and luminous points of an object...; *and the spectator's imagination, experiencing in turn this despotic prompting of the memory*, sees distinctly and vividly the impression produced by things on the mind of Monsieur Guys. The spectator here is the translator of a translation."

The translator of a translation: the expression is wonderfully apt. But it must be understood in its true sense. No more than the painter does the critic content himself with giving a slavish copy. He does not reproduce (how could he reproduce?) the forms and colors of the picture that interests him. But these forms and colors become for him a language, one that depicts a host of feelings and ideas, a whole imaginative life of which he strives to find the equivalent within himself. To the inner life of the painter, enshrined in his picture, corresponds another inner life, it too rooted in an individual past—the inner life of the critic. One becomes the counterpart of the other. Each echoes the other.

Art is therefore doubly capable of prompting the memory. To the painter and the poet, it recalls some past experience which they may avail themselves of as the subject matter of their work; to the spectator and the critic, it recalls a corresponding personal experience.

The best critic is the one who is able to summon up within himself a kind of analogical counterpart of the work that he has read or seen. Such is the essential movement of Baudelaire's thought. Even where he does not look at a work with a deliberately critical or appraising eye, even when (as is often the case) he is looking in it for a source of personal inspiration, even then he cannot prevent his imagination from visualizing what it is that that work creates, from conjuring up as it were an echo or reflection of the work that he admired. So it is that between the latter and his own work there are apt to be similarities, in some cases so striking that Baudelaire himself, afterwards reading over his own writings, hardly knows where to draw the dividing line between what he has gleaned from others and what is the product of his own originality. Speaking of his essay on *Les Paradis artificiels* and in particular of the second part of that essay, in which he closely modelled his work on De Quincey, Baudelaire acknowledged that to his translation he "added here and there his own reflections." But, he had to admit, "just how far I have *introduced my own personality* into the original author, that is something I would now be at a loss to say."

Baudelaire felt much the same uncertainty in connection with all the writers who exerted an influence on him. When he first began reading Edgar Allan Poe, he experienced "a singular commotion." Between Poe's writings and his own he saw a *"close resemblance."* It was this resemblance that chiefly mattered to him, and this it was, as soon as he became aware of it, that impelled him to revert continually to Poe and to take him as his master and inspirer. Yet before he had read a line of him he was already writing poems so much like Poe's that they might have been taken for translations. Why then should he have set so much store by Poe and his writings, since he already possessed in his own right all that they had revealed to him? The answer is simple. If Baudelaire continually reverted to Poe, it was not because Poe had anything new to give him; it was on the contrary because he found in Poe the equivalent of what he found in himself. Poe was his *counterpart*, a second self with whom he maintained relations of symmetry and similarity.

With Baudelaire the act of creation nearly always depended on a mirror effect, on some resemblance detected by him between his own imagination and that of another artist. One day he conceived the idea of writing some prose poems. He discovered a certain correspondence between what he had in mind and the famous *Gaspard de la Nuit* by Aloysius Bertrand. In reading this book over, it occurred to him, he says, to "attempt something *analogous*." It matters little that the resulting book, *Spleen de Paris*, turned out to be a quite different type of work. The important thing is that Baudelaire found his starting point in an analogy. Another example. Rereading the poetry of Marceline Desbordes-Valmore, Baudelaire saw it again with the eyes of the adolescent he had been when he read it for the first time. He rediscovered in the dreams of his boyish days the counterpart of the dreams of the poetess herself. It was not just a matter of some chance similarity, tamely accepted and leading to no results. Baudelaire's imagination *had to act* on this resemblance and transform it into a metaphorical equivalent: "I dream," he wrote, "of what the poetry of Madame Valmore made me feel when I ran through it with those boyish eyes which, in highly-strung men, are at once so ardent and so clairvoyant." This is the attitude, still passive and receptive, of the mere reader. But then comes the transformation of the reader's attitude into an act of criticism: "This poetry," adds Baudelaire, "appears to me like a garden"—a romantic English garden with shady walks whose turnings "open on to far-flung vistas of the past and the future."

Far-flung vistas! It is hardly necessary to point out the analogy between the depths Baudelaire *read into* the poetry of Marceline Desbordes-Valmore and the depths which are so essential a feature of his own poetry. In reading Valmore and visualizing her frail genius, Baudelaire once again found the means of metaphorically visualizing his own genius; or rather of discovering the essential trait in common between him and her, and this, by giving him a deeper insight into another personality, deepened his understanding of his own mind. Baudelaire proceeded in the same way with the painters of whom he has given us an unforgettable critical interpretation in his *Salons*. Taken together or one by one, and seen from a certain angle, they offer a series of metaphorical equivalents of the Baudelairean world.

That world appears then not as a solitary unit reduced to a single train of thought, but as a world preceded, enriched and sustained by a whole procession of kindred spirits and precursors who had already given like-minded versions of it. Baudelaire, so tragically isolated in his private life, thus surrounded himself in his mental life with poets and artists. He surrounded himself with *kindred spirits*. It is these that he called his *"phares"*, his beacons. Along a coast at night great beams of light can be seen flashing through the dark from a number of scattered points. Each stands alone, yet they are interrelated because each is like the other. For Baudelaire great artists and great poets are like beams of light set out at irregular intervals but visible to each other, and together constituting a chain over which the mind makes it way, link by link, noting how each resembles the other. For him these "beacons" were part of the immense universal analogy which he discerned between his own mind and the world, between his own thought and the thought of his forerunners—all, one after another, working the rich veins of analogical truth. And since that truth is revealed not directly but by incessant reflections and reverberations of itself in a succession of mirrors and echoes, it is not surprising that Baudelaire's work should seem to constitute an utterance unceasingly reverted to and unceasingly retransmitted, ringing through a thousand caverns and re-echoed by a thousand voices.

HISTORY, SCIENCE, ARTS, LETTERS	YEAR	BAUDELAIRE
Diderot's first *Salon* published in Grimm's *Correspondance*.	1759	June 7: Birth of Joseph-François Baudelaire, the poet's father, at La Neuville-au-Pont (Marne).
January 21: Execution of Louis XVI.	1793	September 27: Birth in London of Caroline Archenbaut-Defayis (or Archimbaut-Dufays), the poet's mother. Orphaned, she becomes the ward in 1800 of Pierre Pérignon, a friend of François Baudelaire.
Chateaubriand: *Essai sur les Révolutions*.	1797	May 7: Marriage of François Baudelaire with Jeanne-Justine-Rosalie Janin.
	1805	January 18: Birth at Fontainebleau of Claude-Alphonse Baudelaire, the poet's half-brother, who became a magistrate. In 1829 he married Anne-Félicité Ducessois, whom the poet flirted with when he was about twenty-five.
Publication of André Chénier's *Œuvres*, edited by Henri De Latouche. Scott: *Ivanhoe*. Géricault: *The Raft of the Medusa*.	1819	September 9: François Baudelaire, a widower since 1814, marries Caroline Archimbaut-Dufays.
D'Arlincourt: *Le Solitaire*. Joseph de Maistre: *Les Soirées de Saint-Pétersbourg*. Thomas De Quincey: *Confessions of an English Opium-Eater*.	1821	April 9: Birth in Paris, Rue Hautefeuille, of Charles-Pierre Baudelaire.
Delacroix exhibits at the Salon his *Barque of Dante*, which meets with a storm of criticism. Delécluze calls it a "daub." Only Thiers spoke of it with enthusiasm. Hieroglyphics deciphered by Champollion.	1822	April 7: Birth at Mézières, of Aglaé-Joséphine Savatier, illegitimate daughter of Vicomte d'Abancourt; she was known as Apollonie Sabatier before being nicknamed "La Présidente."
Victor Hugo: *Ode à la Colonne ; Cromwell*. Stendhal: *Armance*.	1827	February 10: Death of François Baudelaire. September 30: Birth of Marie Bruneau, called Marie Daubrun, who made her début in 1845 at the Théâtre-Montmartre (today Théâtre de l'Atelier) and later acted at the Vaudeville theater.
Nerval: Translation of *Faust* (Part I).	1828	November 8: Baudelaire's widowed mother marries Major James Aupick (born 1789).
February 25: Uproar over Hugo's *Hernani*. July Revolution: Triumph of the liberal bourgeoisie. Auguste Comte: *Cours de philosophie positive*. Stendhal: *Le Rouge et le Noir*.	1830	
	1831	December: Lt. Col. Aupick appointed Chief of Staff of the 7th Division at Lyons.
April-July: Cholera epidemic in Paris, with over 18,000 victims. Death of Goethe and of Cuvier: Mickiewicz in Paris. Corot: *Bath of Diana*.	1832	January: Charles and his mother join Aupick in Lyons, where Charles enters the first form at the Pension Delorme. October: Charles enters the Collège Royal of Lyons as a boarder.

HISTORY, SCIENCE, ARTS, LETTERS	YEAR	BAUDELAIRE
Balzac: *Eugénie Grandet.* Hugo: *Lucrèce Borgia; Marie Tudor.* George Sand: *Lélia.*	1833	
April: Insurrection in Lyons and Paris. Sainte-Beuve: *Volupté.* Delacroix: *Women of Algiers.*	1834	For his services in putting down the insurrection in Lyons, Aupick is promoted full Colonel.
Thiers Ministry.	1836	Aupick appointed Chief of Staff of the Paris garrison. On March 1, Charles enters the fourth form at the Collège Louis-le-Grand, Paris.
Théophile Gautier: *La Comédie de la mort.*	1838	Late August to early October: Journey in the Pyrenees with his parents which later inspired the poem *Incompatibilité.*
Petrus Borel: *Madame Putiphar.* Balzac: *Béatrix; Un grand homme de province à Paris.*	1839	April 18: Dismissed from the Collège Louis-le-Grand for refusing to hand over a note passed to him by a schoolfellow. August: Aupick promoted to the rank of General; Charles passes his *baccalauréat.*
December: Ashes of Napoleon returned to France. Hugo: *Les Rayons et les Ombres.* Musset: *Poésies complètes.* Sainte-Beuve: *Poésies complètes.* Proudhon: *Qu'est-ce que la propriété?*	1840	At the Pension Bailly, 11 Place de l'Estrapade, Paris, Baudelaire meets Gustave Le Vavasseur and Ernest Prarond. Liaison with Sarah, called Louchette, a Latin Quarter prostitute who inspired several poems: *"Je n'ai pas pour maîtresse une lionne illustre...," "Une nuit que j'étais près d'une affreuse juive...", "Tu mettrais l'univers entier dans ta ruelle..."*
	1841	June: To put a stop to his irregular way of life, his family arrange to send him on a voyage to the East, and at Bordeaux he boards the *Paquebot-des-Mers-du-Sud*, bound for Calcutta. September: Sojourn on the island of Mauritius. October: Baudelaire refuses to go further than Bourbon Island and boards the *Alcide* for the voyage home.
Tahiti becomes a French protectorate. End of the Opium War in China. Balzac: Preface to *La Comédie Humaine.* Théodore de Banville: Brilliant start with *Les Cariatides.* Aloysius Bertrand: *Gaspard de la Nuit* (edited by Sainte-Beuve and Victor Pavie). Eugène Sue: *Les Mystères de Paris* published serially in *La Presse.*	1842	February: Arrival in Bordeaux and return to Paris. Soon after, Baudelaire meets Jeanne Duval, with whom he remained on intimate terms for most of his life. She inspired many poems, including: *"Je t'adore à l'égal de la voûte nocturne...", "Avec ses vêtements ondoyants et nacrés...", Le Chat, Le Balcon, Un Fantôme.* April 9: Baudelaire comes of age and enters into possession of the fortune bequeathed to him by his father (70,000 francs). June: He moves into an apartment in the Ile Saint-Louis, 10 Quai de Béthune.

HISTORY, SCIENCE, ARTS, LETTERS	YEAR	BAUDELAIRE
January 24: Revival of *Phèdre* at the Comédie-Française with Rachel: a great success. March 7: Failure of Victor Hugo's *Burgraves*. April 22: Success of Ponsard's neo-classical tragedy *Lucrèce*.	1843	February: Publication of a book of poems, *Vers*, by Gustave Le Vavasseur, Ernest Prarond and A. Argonne (pseudonym of Auguste Dozon). It has been shown by Jules Mouquet that Baudelaire collaborated anonymously on the second part of the book. About the same time he has a share in a verse drama, *Idéolus*, of which the manuscript is mostly in Prarond's hand. May: Moves to the Hôtel Pimodan. In the studio of the painter Ferdinand Boissard de Boisdenier he meets Gautier, perhaps Apollonie Sabatier and Balzac; there too he meets the members of the Hashish Club met. Runs into debt with Arondel, a second-hand dealer who sells him fake Poussins, Tintorettos, Correggios, Velazquezes, etc. It was probably in 1843 that Baudelaire sent Sainte-Beuve an admiring letter and a verse epistle.
French conquest of Algeria: Battle of Isly. Political refugees found in Paris the "Young Europe" party, organized by Mazzini. Balzac: *Modeste Mignon; Un début dans la vie; Honorine*. Chateaubriand: *Vie de Rancé*. Dumas: *Les Trois Mousquetaires*. Nerval: *Le Christ aux Oliviers* (in *L'Artiste*, March 31). Vigny: *La Maison du Berger* (in *Revue des Deux Mondes*, July 15). Eugène Sue: *Le Juif errant* (serial publication in *Journal des Débats*).	1844	March 2: Publication of *Les Mystères galans des Théâtres de Paris*, an anonymous collection of gossip and anecdotes contributed by Mathieu-Dairnvaell, Fortuné Mesuré, Privat d'Anglemont, Abbé Constant and Baudelaire (author in particular of a diatribe against Ponsard). July: Alarmed by her son's extravagance, Madame Aupick takes steps to have his estate administered by a guardian. September 21: The civil court designates Narcisse-Désiré Ancelle, notary public at Neuilly, as Baudelaire's guardian. The poet suffered all his life from this humiliation, but in the end, after having cursed him, did justice to his guardian.
Gautier: *España*. Mérimée: *Carmen*.	1845	April: Publication of the *Salon de 1845*. On the back cover, *De la peinture moderne* is announced as "in the press," and *De la caricature, David, Guérin, Girodet* as "forthcoming." May 25: The sonnet *A une Dame créole* published in *L'Artiste*. June 30: To Ancelle, Baudelaire announces his intention of committing suicide; he bequeathes his belongings to Jeanne Duval, his papers to Banville. The attempt miscarried, his scratch soon healed, and he lived for a while with his parents. October: On the cover of *L'Agiotage*, a satire by Pierre Dupont, a book of poems by Baudelaire entitled *Les Lesbiennes* is announced as forthcoming; the same announcement appears on the covers of several other books in 1846 and 1847. He later changed the title to *Les Limbes*; it finally appeared as *Les Fleurs du Mal*.

HISTORY, SCIENCE, ARTS, LETTERS	YEAR	BAUDELAIRE
Banville: *Les Stalactites*. Nerval: *Voyage en Orient* published in part in *Revue des Deux Mondes*.	1846	February: *Le Jeune Enchanteur* appears under Baudelaire's name in *L'Esprit public*. It has recently been shown by W. T. Bandy that this was actually an adaptation of an English story by the Reverend George Croly (1836). March 3: *Le Corsaire-Satan* publishes a *Choix de Maximes consolantes sur l'amour* and announces a forthcoming *Catéchisme de la femme aimée* (never published). April 15: *Conseils aux jeunes littérateurs* in *L'Esprit public*.
May 10: Death of the painter Emile Deroy. September: Emile Daurand-Forgues sends in to the *Revue britannique* a French translation of Poe's *Descent into the Maelstrom*. October: Forgues' translation of Poe's *Murders in the Rue Morgue* published in *Le Commerce*. Study of Poe in *Revue des Deux Mondes*.		May: The *Salon de 1846* goes on sale.
January 27: Isabelle Meunier publishes a translation of Poe's *Black Cat* in *La Démocratie pacifique*. It was this story, according to Asselineau, that revealed Poe's work to Baudelaire. Béranger: *Œuvres complètes*. Michelet: *Histoire de la Révolution française*, Vol. I. Louis Blanc: *Histoire de la Révolution française*, Vol. I. Lamartine: *Histoire des Girondins*.	1847	January: *La Fanfarlo* appears in the *Bulletin de la Société des gens de lettres*. November: Aupick appointed Commandant of the Ecole Polytechnique. Portrait of Baudelaire by Courbet; beginning of their friendship.
February Revolution in Paris. June insurrection. December 10: Louis-Napoléon elected President of the Republic. Dumas *fils*: *La Dame aux camélias* (novel). July 4: Death of Chateaubriand; his *Mémoires d'outre-tombe* published serially in *La Presse*.	1848	February 24: Baudelaire on the barricades. With Champfleury and Toubin, he founds *Le Salut public*, which folds up after two issues (February 27 and March 1 or 2). April 10 to May 6: Baudelaire edits *La Tribune nationale*, a moderate republican paper. April 13: Aupick appointed Minister of the French Republic at Constantinople.
Flaubert and Maxime Du Camp travel together through Greece, Syria and Egypt. Sainte-Beuve: Monday literary column *(Lundi)* in *Le Constitutionnel*, then in *Le Moniteur*, then in *Le Temps*.	1849	October 7: Death of Edgar Allan Poe in Baltimore. First contacts with the publisher Poulet-Malassis. December: Mysterious visit to Dijon.
Ponsard: *Charlotte Corday*. George Sand: *François Le Champi*. Mérimée: *H.B.* (on Stendhal). Extra tax on papers that publish serial novels.	1850	Asselineau remembers having seen at Baudelaire's "the manuscript of his poems beautifully copied by a calligrapher, and bound in two quarto volumes with gilt lettering. From this manuscript the *Fleurs du Mal* was printed." This all-important manuscript has never come to light. June: *L'Ame du Vin* and *Châtiment de l'Orgueil* published in *Le Magasin des Familles*, where they are presented as excerpts from a forthcoming volume entitled *Les Limbes*.

HISTORY, SCIENCE, ARTS, LETTERS	YEAR	BAUDELAIRE
Barbey d'Aurevilly: *Une vieille maîtresse.* Henri Murger: *Le Pays latin ; Scènes de la vie de Bohème.*	1851	March 7-12: *Du vin et du hachish comparés comme moyens de multiplication de l'individu,* initial version of the first part of *Les Paradis artificiels,* published in the *Messager de l'Assemblée.* April 9: Publication in the same paper of eleven poems under the title *Les Limbes.* Baudelaire, who had made himself a reputation as an unpublished poet, breaks silence. June 18: Aupick appointed French Ambassador at Madrid, where he remains until April 1853. August: Laudatory article on Pierre Dupont. October: Baudelaire orders Poe's works from London.
December 2: Coup d'état of Louis-Napoléon Bonaparte, who assumes the title of Emperor of the French.		November 27: *La Semaine théâtrale* publishes an article against Augier and Ponsard: *L'Ecole du bon sens.*
Second Republic changed into the Second Empire by Napoleon III. Gautier: *Emaux et Camées.* Leconte de Lisle: *Poèmes antiques.* Nerval: *Lorély.* Victor Hugo: *Napoléon le Petit.*	1852	January 22: *L'Ecole païenne,* an article aimed at Banville and also perhaps at Ménard, Gautier, Leconte de Lisle and Victor de Laprade, published in *La Semaine théâtrale.* March-April: Baudelaire publishes *Edgar Allan Poe, sa vie et ses ouvrages* in the *Revue de Paris.* About two thirds of this article come from a review of Poe's works by John M. Daniel published in the *Southern Literary Messenger* in 1850. December 9: Baudelaire's first (unsigned) letter to Madame Sabatier, sending her the poem *A celle qui est trop gaie.*
Marriage of Napoleon III with Eugénie de Montijo. Haussmann appointed Prefect of the Seine. Beginning of the Crimean War. Champfleury: *Les souffrances du Professeur Deltheil ; Les Aventures de Mlle Mariette* (realist novels). Nerval: *Petits châteaux de Bohème.* Taine: *Essai sur les Fables de La Fontaine.* Gobineau: *Essai sur l'inégalité des races humaines,* Vol. I. November: Victor Hugo publishes *Les Châtiments* in Brussels.	1853	March 1: Translation of Poe's *Raven* in *L'Artiste.* March 8: Aupick made Senator of the Empire. March 27: Translation of Poe's *Philosophy of Furniture* in *Le Monde littéraire.* May 3 and 9: Letters to Madame Sabatier with the poems *Réversibilité* and *Confession.*
February 1: Vigny's poem *La Bouteille à la mer* in *Revue des Deux Mondes.* Nerval: *Les Filles du Feu.* Augier and Sandeau: *Le Gendre de M. Poirier* (comedy).	1854	February 7: To Madame Sabatier he sends *Le Flambeau vivant* and, a few days later, *L'Aube spirituelle.* February 16: He sends her the sonnet *"Que diras-tu ce soir..."* May 8: He sends her the *Hymne* which was only to be published in *Les Epaves* (1866). July 25: *Le Pays* begins publishing his translation of Poe's romances (continued until April 20, 1855).

HISTORY, SCIENCE, ARTS, LETTERS	YEAR	BAUDELAIRE
January 26: Gérard de Nerval found dead by hanging in the Rue de la Vieille-Lanterne. Maxime Du Camp: *Chants modernes.* Champfleury: *Les Bourgeois de Molinchart* (realist novel of provincial life). June 28: Opening of the Courbet exhibition entitled "Realism."	1855	May 26 to August 12: Publication in *Le Pays*, then in *Le Portefeuille* of three articles on the Paris World's Fair. June 1: Baudelaire publishes 18 poems in *Revue des Deux Mondes* under the title *Les Fleurs du Mal* (according to Asselineau, this title was suggested by Hippolyte Babou). First prose poems (*Le Crépuscule du Soir* and *La Solitude*) in *Hommage to Denecourt.*
Congress and Treaty of Paris. Hugo: *Les Contemplations.* Tocqueville: *L'Ancien Régime et la Révolution.* Flaubert's *Madame Bovary* published in the *Revue de Paris;* legal action taken against the author who is acquitted.	1856	March 12: First volume of Baudelaire's translation of Poe, *Histoires extraordinaires*, goes on sale.
Banville: *Odes funambulesques.* Glatigny: *Les Vignes folles.* Champfleury: *La Succession de Le Camus* (realist novel). Fromentin: *Un été dans le Sahara.* *Le Réalisme*, a magazine edited by Duranty and Champfleury, published from July 1856 to May 1857 (six issues).	1857	February 4: Manuscript of *Les Fleurs du Mal* delivered to the Paris correspondant of Poulet-Malassis. March 8: Second volume of Baudelaire's translation of Poe, *Nouvelles histoires extraordinaires*, goes on sale. April 28: Death of General Aupick. June 21: Publication of *Les Fleurs du Mal.* July 5: The *Fleurs du Mal* reviewed by Bourdin in *Le Figaro.* It was probably this foolish and spiteful review that drew the public prosecutor's attention to the book. July 11: Baudelaire informs Poulet-Malassis of the confiscation of all copies on sale in Paris and asks him to hide the remainder of the edition. July 14: Laudatory review by Edouard Thierry in *Le Moniteur.* July 18: Baudelaire asks Madame Sabatier to intercede with the judges who are to decide his case. August 20: Case against the *Fleurs du Mal* heard before the 6th Chambre Correctionnelle in Paris. Indictment by Ernest Pinard who had presented the case against *Madame Bovary.* Speech for the defense by Me Chaix d'Est-Ange. Judgment returned against author and publisher who are fined and ordered to withdraw six poems from the book. August 24: A series of six prose poems under the title *Poèmes nocturnes* published in *Le Présent.* August 30: Madame Sabatier yields to Baudelaire. October 1 and 15: *Le Présent* publishes Baudelaire's studies of French and foreign caricaturists (written in 1844-1848). October 18: Review of *Madame Bovary* in *Le Présent.*

HISTORY, SCIENCE, ARTS, LETTERS	YEAR	BAUDELAIRE
Asselineau: *La Double Vie,* a book of stories whose preface was revised by Baudelaire. Gautier: *Le Roman de la Momie.* Ernest Feydeau: *Fanny,* a novel compared at the time with *Madame Bovary* and praised by Sainte-Beuve.	1858	May 13: Baudelaire's third volume of Poe translations, *Les Aventures d'Arthur Gordon Pym,* goes on sale; it had been serialized the year before in *Le Moniteur Universel.* September 30: *Le Hachish,* first part of *Les Paradis artificiels,* appears in the *Revue contemporaine.* October: Short stay with his mother at Honfleur.
Amnesty granted by Napoleon III to political convicts. Work begins on the Suez Canal. Hugo: *La Légende des Siècles* (1st series). Darwin: *Origin of Species.* J.M. de Heredia begins publishing his sonnets in magazines. François-Victor Hugo begins his translation of Shakespeare, working on it until 1865.	1859	January-February: Another stay at Honfleur. Writing of his longest poem, *Le Voyage* (printed in placard form). January 9: Review of Asselineau's *La Double Vie* published in *L'Artiste.* March 13: *L'Artiste* publishes Baudelaire's study of Gautier, at once reprinted as a booklet with a letter-preface by Victor Hugo, who speaks of the *"frisson nouveau,"* the new thrill, created by the *Fleurs du Mal.* April 5: Jeanne Duval, stricken with paralysis, enters the Hôpital Dubois where she stays until May 19. April 20: The *Revue française* publishes *La Genèse d'un poème* (a new translation of *The Raven*), from the *Philosophy of Composition.* May-June: Another stay at Honfleur. June-July: Publication of the *Salon de 1859* in the *Revue française.* October: The *Revue internationale* in Geneva begins publishing Poe's *Eureka* translated by Baudelaire, but it is discontinued.
December: Death of Thomas De Quincey at Edinburgh.		December: Another stay at Honfleur.
Savoy and Nice ceded to France by the Kingdom of Piedmont. Cavour invades the Papal States. Labiche: *Le voyage de M. Perrichon.* Edmond and Jules de Goncourt: *Les hommes de lettres* (retitled *Charles Demailly* in 1868). Duranty: *Le Malheur d'Henriette Gérard* (realist novel).	1860	January 1: New contract between Baudelaire and Poulet-Malassis for a second edition of *Les Fleurs du Mal, Les Paradis artificiels,* and *Opinions littéraires* (the last published posthumously as *Art romantique* and *Curiosités esthétiques,* titles chosen by Asselineau and Banville). January 15 and 31: *Un mangeur d'opium,* second part of *Les Paradis artificiels,* published in the *Revue contemporaine.* April 17: Long letter to Richard Wagner in which Baudelaire expresses his admiration. Late May: *Les Paradis artificiels* published in book form by Poulet-Malassis.
Emile Augier: *Les Effrontés* (society comedy). Michelet: *La Mer.* Sainte-Beuve: *Chateaubriand et son groupe littéraire sous l'Empire* (Liège lectures 1848-1849). Salon of 1861: Manet exhibits his *Guitarrero.*	1861	February: Publication of the second edition of *Les Fleurs du Mal.* April 1: Study of *Richard Wagner et Tannhäuser à Paris* in the *Revue européenne,* then in booklet form. To his mother Baudelaire announces his intention of writing a confession to be called *Mon cœur mis à nu,* which has been in his mind for two years past; only notes for it were written.

HISTORY, SCIENCE, ARTS, LETTERS	YEAR	BAUDELAIRE
	1861	May 24: Baudelaire sells to Poulet-Malassis and de Broise the exclusive right to publish his works.
		June-August: The *Revue fantaisiste*, recently founded by young Catulle Mendès, publishes Baudelaire's *Réflexions sur quelques-uns de mes contemporains* (Hugo, Barbier, Marceline Desbordes-Valmore, Gautier, Petrus Borel, Banville, Pierre Dupont, Leconte de Lisle, Gustave Le Vavasseur).
		November 1: The *Revue fantaisiste* publishes another series of prose poems, nine in all (three of them new).
		December: Baudelaire's candidature for the Académie Française. Two seats were vacant, Lacordaire's and Scribe's; the poet became a candidate for the first. This step created a scandal and his friends, especially Sainte-Beuve, advised him to withdraw, which he did on February 10, 1862. This abortive venture won him, however, the friendship of Alfred de Vigny.
French expedition to Mexico. Garibaldi's abortive attempt to take Rome. Bismarck minister-president of Prussia. Leconte de Lisle: *Poèmes barbares.* Hugo: *Les Misérables,* favorably reviewed by Baudelaire in *Le Boulevard* of April 20, which did not prevent him from describing the novel in a letter to his mother as *"immonde et inepte"* (foul and inept.) Duranty: *La Cause du beau Guillaume.* Villiers de L'Isle-Adam: *Isis.* September 6: In London, *The Spectator* publishes an enthusiastic article by Swinburne on *Les Fleurs du Mal*; the English poet becomes one of the first of Baudelaire's disciples.	1862	January 23: Baudelaire makes the following entry in *Fusées*: "I have cultivated my hysteria with relish and terror... today, January 23, 1862, I felt pass over me the fluttering wing of imbecility." April 14: Death at Fontainebleau of Claude-Alphonse Baudelaire, the poet's half-brother. August 26-27 and September 24: *La Presse* publishes the first 20 prose poems, with a dedication in the form of a letter to Arsène Houssaye. The fourth instalment containing pieces XXI to XXVI, was canceled at the proof stage because Baudelaire combined some previously published pieces with the new ones. November: Bankruptcy of Poulet-Malassis, who soon takes refuge in Belgium.
Renan: *La Vie de Jésus.* Fromentin: *Dominique.* Louis Ménard: *Le Polythéisme hellénique.* Littré: *Dictionnaire de la langue française*, Vol. I (Vol. IV in 1868). Salon of 1863: Manet's *Déjeuner sur l'Herbe* creates a scandal.	1863	January 13: Baudelaire sells to the publisher Hetzel the exclusive publishing rights in the *Fleurs du Mal* and the *Petits Poèmes en prose* which he had already sold to Poulet-Malassis. June-December: Seven new prose poems published in the *Revue nationale et étrangère.* August 13: Death of Delacroix. Obituary study by Baudelaire in *L'Opinion nationale* (September and November). November 26, 29, and December 3: *Le Peintre de la vie moderne* published in *Le Figaro.*

HISTORY, SCIENCE, ARTS, LETTERS	YEAR	BAUDELAIRE
Vigny: Posthumous publication of *Les Destinées*. Austro-Prussian war against Denmark. First International founded by Marx. Creation of the Comité des Forges. Léon Dierx: *Poèmes et poésies*. Meilhac and Halévy: *La Belle Hélène* (music by Offenbach). Edmond and Jules de Goncourt: *Mademoiselle Mauperin*. Barbey d'Aurevilly: *Le Chevalier Des Touches*. Fustel de Coulanges: *La Cité antique*. Pierre Larousse: *Grand Dictionnaire Universel du XIXe siècle*, Vol. I (Vol. XVII in 1876).	1864	February 7 and 14: Six prose poems published under the title *Le Spleen de Paris* in *Le Figaro*. April 24: Baudelaire leaves for Brussels, where he hopes to find a publisher for his complete works and to earn some money by lecturing. He stays at the Hôtel du Grand Miroir. May-June: Five lectures on Delacroix, Gautier, and *Les Paradis artificiels*. Not very successful; his fee is less than promised. He begins writing notes for a pamphlet against Belgium. During the summer he visits the principal Belgian cities. December 25: Six new prose poems under the title *Le Spleen de Paris* published in the *Revue de Paris*.
Abolition of slavery in the United States. International Telegraph Union. February 1: *L'Artiste* publishes Mallarmé's *Symphonie littéraire*, the second part of which is devoted to Baudelaire. November 16, 30, and December 23: *L'Art* publishes a long article by Verlaine on Baudelaire, who is more irritated than flattered by it. Hugo: *Chansons des rues et des bois*. Barbey d'Aurevilly: *Un prêtre marié*. Zola: *La Confession de Claude*. Taine: *Philosophie de l'Art*. Claude Bernard: *Introduction à la médecine expérimentale*. Salon of 1865: Manet exhibits *Olympia*.	1865	February: A rancorous article by Jules Janin on *Henri Heine et la Jeunesse des Poètes*, published in *L'Indépendance belge*, provokes a cutting reply from Baudelaire; but the reply was never sent in and only two drafts have survived. Increasingly unwell. July 4-15: Short trip to Paris and Honfleur.
Austria defeated by Prussia at Sadowa. Sully Prudhomme: *Les Epreuves*. Verlaine: *Poèmes saturniens*. Coppée: *Le Reliquaire*. Hugo: *Les Travailleurs de la Mer*. Dostoevsky: *Crime and Punishment*. Zola: *Le Vœu d'une morte; Mes haines; Mon Salon*. Veuillot: *Les Odeurs de Paris*. Leconte de Lisle: Translation of the *Iliad* and, the following year, the *Odyssey*.	1866	Early February: Baudelaire consults his mother and Asselineau about his illness which is getting worse daily. Late February: Publication of *Les Epaves*. Mid-March: Baudelaire collapses while visiting the church of Saint-Loup at Namur with Félicien Rops. First symptoms of aphasia and hemiplegia. March 31: Fifteen poems published in the *Parnasse contemporain* under the title *Nouvelles Fleurs du Mal*. July 2: Baudelaire, who has not recovered the power of speech but whose other faculties are unimpaired, is brought back to Paris by his mother and the painter Arthur Stevens. Placed in the nursing home of Dr Duval, he is visited there by Sainte-Beuve, Maxime Du Camp, Théodore de Banville, Leconte de Lisle and Nadar; Madame Paul Meurice comes and plays Wagner for him.

HISTORY, SCIENCE, ARTS, LETTERS	YEAR	BAUDELAIRE
Liberal concessions made by Napoleon III. Banville: *Les Exilés*. Meilhac and Halévy: *La Vie parisienne*. Zola: *Thérèse Raquin*. Karl Marx: *Das Kapital*.	1867	August 31: Death of Baudelaire. On the same day the *Revue nationale et étrangère* begins publication of a final series of *Petits poèmes en prose*.
Lautréamont: *Les Chants de Maldoror*, Canto I. Zola: *La Honte* (serialized in *L'Evénement*).	1868	December: The publishing firm of Lévy brings out the first volumes of Baudelaire's *Œuvres complètes*, prefaced by Théophile Gautier and edited by Asselineau and Banville. Running to seven volumes, the edition was completed in 1870. Reprinted several times up to 1917, when Baudelaire's works came into the public domain.
Opening of the Suez Canal. Socialist Congress at Basel. Banville: *Nouvelles Odes funambulesques*. Sully Prudhomme: *Les Solitudes*. Verlaine: *Fêtes galantes*. Meilhac and Halévy: *Froufrou*. Hugo: *L'Homme qui rit*. Flaubert: *L'Education sentimentale*.	1869	First biography of Baudelaire, by his friend Charles Asselineau, brought out by Lemerre, publisher of the Parnassians (Leconte de Lisle, Banville, Sully Prudhomme, Heredia).
Lautréamont: *Poésies*. Taine: *De l'intelligence*. Franco-Prussian War: Defeat of France and collapse of the Second Empire. Victor Hugo returns to France.	1870	Nadar catches sight of Jeanne Duval for the last time, dragging herself along on crutches.
Paris Commune.	1871	August 16: Death of Madame Aupick.

The number of books and articles inspired by the life and writings of Baudelaire is far larger than those devoted to any other French writer. In 1954 the Rimbaud bibliography compiled by ETIEMBLE numbered nearly 3,500 items. At that time the Baudelaire bibliography on which W.T. BANDY had been working for forty years was twice as long. (It may be pointed out here that, on the initiative of W.T. BANDY, a Center of Baudelaire Studies has just been founded at Vanderbilt University, Nashville, Tennessee, and is already publishing a *Baudelaire Bulletin*.) When it is published, this bibliography will contain over 10,000 items—a monument raised to the glory of Baudelaire, but also to that of human Stupidity, the "bull-browed Stupidity" of several generations of critics. For this enormous mass of commentary and exegesis can be boiled down to about a hundred books and some two hundred articles: these contain the essential. There can be no question of enumerating them all here. The following summary will provide sufficient orientation for the interested reader and the student of Baudelaire.

Introductory Books

The most complete and perceptive presentation is M.A. RUFF, *Baudelaire*, Connaissance des Lettres, Hatier, Paris 1955 (reprinted and brought up to date in 1967). — *Baudelaire par lui-même* by Pascal PIA (Les Ecrivains de toujours, Editions du Seuil, Paris 1952) gives a vivid portrait of the young Baudelaire. A German translation has been published in the series of Rowohlts Monographien (Hamburg 1958).

Editions

a) *Complete Works*

Three new editions of the *Oeuvres complètes* were published in 1967 and 1968 to commemorate the centenary of Baudelaire's death: by Yves FLORENNE (Club français du Livre, Paris, 3 vols.), by Marcel RAYMOND (Guilde du Livre, Lausanne, 1 vol.), and by M.A. RUFF (L'Intégrale, Editions du Seuil, Paris, 1 vol.). All three are based on earlier editions. That of Yves FLORENNE follows the edition produced by Claude PICHOIS for the Club du Meilleur Livre (Paris 1955, 2 vols.), which for the first time printed the texts in the chronological order of publication. For that chronology of publication, however, Yves FLORENNE tries to substitute a chronology of composition, which inevitably leads to misgivings and uncertainties. What is more, he prints not the text of the second edition of *Les Fleurs du Mal* (1861) but that of the first (1857). The editions of Marcel RAYMOND and Marcel A. RUFF are based on that edited by Y.G. LE DANTEC and Claude PICHOIS for the Pléiade series (Gallimard, Paris 1961, 5th revised and corrected printing, 1968). The originality of Marcel RAYMOND's edition lies in the sound and discerning prefaces with which the editor has headed each section of the book. — Specialists must always refer to the large edition in 19 volumes edited by Jacques CRÉPET and Claude PICHOIS (Conard-Lambert, Paris 1922-1953); this is the standard edition. It alone provides the *Correspondance générale* of the poet, which has been added to recently by a volume of *Lettres inédites aux siens* (Grasset, Paris 1966) whose editing, however, falls short of scholarly standards (Italian translation by Luigi DE NARDIS, Rizzoli, Milan 1968; German translation by Alfred SCHELZIG, Walter Verlag, Olten 1969).

b) *Critical Editions*

These are few in number. The following may be mentioned: *Les Fleurs du Mal*, edited by Jacques CRÉPET and Georges BLIN (José Corti, Paris 1942; 2nd edition, 1950). A complete revision of this edition is being prepared by Georges BLIN and Claude PICHOIS: the first volume, containing the text and all the variants, together with the documents relating to the trial, has just been published (José Corti, Paris 1968); volumes II and III will contain the editors' commentaries. — *Petits Poèmes en prose*, critical edition by Robert KOPP (José Corti, Paris 1969). — *Le Salon de 1845 de Charles Baudelaire*, critical edition with introduction and notes by André FERRAN (Editions de l'Archer, Toulouse 1933). — Critical editions of *Le Salon de 1846* (by David KELLEY) and *Les Paradis artificiels* (by Michèle LIPMAN-WULF) are in preparation.

c) *Other Editions*

These are legion. Only those are listed here which provide the reader with helpful commentaries. — *Les Fleurs du Mal*: edited by Jean POMMIER and Claude PICHOIS, illustrated with pictures which may have inspired the poet (Club des Libraires de France, Paris 1959; reprinted by Editions A. Balland, 1967); edited by Antoine ADAM (Classiques Garnier, Paris 1961); edited by Jean POMMIER (Slatkine Reprints, Geneva 1968, facsimile of the 1857 edition accompanied by a volume of commentaries). — *Petits Poèmes en prose*: edited by Henri LEMAITRE (Classiques Garnier, Paris 1958); edited by Melvin ZIMMERMANN (Manchester University Press, 1968). — *Les Paradis artificiels*: edited by Claude PICHOIS (Club du Meilleur Livre, Paris 1961; reprinted in Le Livre de Poche, Paris 1964; contains not only Baudelaire's text but also Théophile Gautier's writings on opium and hashish, together with a useful introduction). — Critical writings: *Critique littéraire et musicale*, edited by Claude PICHOIS (Bibliothèque de Cluny, Armand Colin, Paris 1961); *Critique d'art*, edited by Claude PICHOIS (Bibliothèque de Cluny, Armand Colin, Paris 1965, 2 vols.); *Curiosités esthétiques* and *L'Art romantique* edited by Henri LEMAITRE (Classiques Garnier, Paris 1962). — Illustrated editions reproducing works of art discussed by Baudelaire: *Baudelaire critique d'art. Curiosités esthétiques, poèmes, œuvres diverses, lettres*, edited by Bernard GHERBRANT (Club des Libraires de France, Paris 1956). Well illustrated and annotated are the three volumes of art criticism translated and edited by Jonathan MAYNE: *The Mirror of Art. Critical Studies by Charles Baudelaire* (Phaidon Press, London 1955), *The Painter of Modern Life and Other Essays by Charles Baudelaire* (Phaidon Press, London 1964), and *Art in Paris, 1845-1862. Salons and Other Exhibitions reviewed by Charles Baudelaire* (Phaidon Press, London 1965).

Bibliographies, Current Reports, Exhibition Catalogues

W.T. BANDY, *Répertoire des écrits sur Baudelaire* (Madison, Wis. 1953), issued in 50 mimeographed copies, listing 5,029 items. The new typewritten version, covering everything published up to 1962, contains over 10,000 items. Since 1963 complete checklists of new publications, prepared by W.T. BANDY, S. PATTY and Peter C. HOY, appear in the *Bulletin baudelairien* (Vanderbilt University, Nashville, Tennessee) founded in 1965 for this purpose. — R.F. CARGO, *Baudelaire Criticism 1950-1967. A Critical Bibliography* (University of North Carolina Press, Chapel Hill 1969).

Henri PEYRE, *Connaissance de Baudelaire* (José Corti, Paris 1951) is a useful introduction to Baudelaire studies, though now inevitably somewhat out of date; it contains a bibliography of 337 items. — Claude PICHOIS, "Esquisse d'un état présent des études baudelairiennes," *L'information littéraire* (Editions Baillière), January-February 1958, pp. 8-17, provides an authoritative summing up and indicates possible lines of research. For a report on the past ten years' work, see Claude PICHOIS, "Pour une prospective baudelairienne," *Etudes Littéraires* (Laval University), Vol. I, No. 1, April 1968, pp. 125-128, and Lloyd James AUSTIN, "Etat présent des études sur Baudelaire," *Forum for Modern Language Studies* (University of St. Andrews), Vol. III, No. 4, October 1967, pp. 352-369. — A comprehensive account of the publications and

festivities of the Baudelaire years 1968-1969, together with an up-to-date review of Baudelaire studies, is being prepared by Claude PICHOIS and Robert KOPP (Editions de la Baconnière, Neuchâtel, Switzerland, forthcoming late 1969).

The centenary of *Les Fleurs du Mal* was commemorated by an exhibition at the Bibliothèque Nationale, Paris (1957), and that of Baudelaire's death by an exhibition at the Petit Palais, Paris (November 1968-March 1969); a catalogue was issued for each exhibition.

Biographies and Iconographies

The standard biography is still that of Eugène and Jacques CRÉPET, *Baudelaire* (Messein, Paris 1906; reprinted several times but now out of print). This is a revised and enlarged version by Jacques CRÉPET (1874-1952) of the study with which his father Eugène CRÉPET (1827-1892) prefaced his edition of Baudelaire's *Oeuvres posthumes* (Quantin, Paris 1887). Although it now calls for correction in some points, this biography nevertheless remains the only one which is accurate in its facts and fair in its judgments.

The contemporary accounts of Baudelaire have been brought together by W.T. BANDY, *Baudelaire judged by his Contemporaries, 1845-1867* (Publication of the Institute of French Studies, Columbia University, New York 1933), and by W.T. BANDY and Claude PICHOIS, *Baudelaire devant ses contemporains* (Editions du Rocher, Monaco 1957; enlarged edition with a new preface by Claude PICHOIS, Union générale d'Edition, Collection 10-18, Paris 1967; German translation with a critical and annotated bibliography of 328 items by Felix INGOLD and Robert KOPP, Insel Verlag, Frankfurt 1969). To these may be added the texts assembled and annotated by Jacques CRÉPET and Claude PICHOIS, *Baudelaire et Asselineau* (Nizet, Paris 1953). — W.T. BANDY's work has been followed up by Alfred Edward CARTER, *Baudelaire et la critique française, 1868-1917* (University of South Carolina Press, Columbia, S.C. 1963).

Certain biographical problems have been the object of detailed studies: Pierre DUFAY, *Autour de Baudelaire. Poulet-Malassis, l'éditeur et l'ami. Madame Sabatier, la muse et la madone* (Au Cabinet du Livre, Paris 1931). While the first part of this book remains useful, the second part has been superseded by André BILLY, *La Présidente* (Flammarion, Paris 1945), a well documented study to which Louis MERMAZ, *Madame Sabatier* (Editions Rencontre, Lausanne 1967) adds nothing new. — Albert FEUILLERAT, *Baudelaire et la belle aux cheveux d'or* (José Corti, Paris; Yale University Press, New Haven 1941). — Albert FEUILLERAT, *Baudelaire et sa mère* (Editions Variétés, Montreal 1944). — Jules MOUQUET and W.T. BANDY, *Baudelaire en 1848* (Emile-Paul frères, Paris 1946). — Claude PICHOIS, *Le vrai visage du général Aupick* (Mercure de France, Paris 1955). — Claude PICHOIS, *Baudelaire à Paris* (Albums littéraires de la France, Hachette, Paris 1967). — Jean URRUTY, *Baudelaire aux Mascareignes* (Port Louis, Mauritius 1968). — See also several articles on Baudelaire's youth and his relations with his friends in Jacques CRÉPET, *Propos sur Baudelaire* (Mercure de France, Paris 1957) and in Claude

PICHOIS, *Baudelaire, Etudes et témoignages* (Editions de la Baconnière, Neuchâtel 1967).

Iconographie de Charles Baudelaire, edited by Claude PICHOIS and François RUCHON (Cailler, Geneva 1960). — For facsimile reproductions of Baudelaire's drawings, see *Dessins de Baudelaire*, foreword by Jacques CRÉPET (Gallimard, Paris 1927).

Essays in Exegesis

a) *General Studies*

Gonzague de REYNOLD, *Charles Baudelaire* (Crès, Paris, and Georg, Geneva 1920). — Ernest RAYNAUD, *Baudelaire* (Garnier, Paris 1922). — Enid STARKIE, *Baudelaire* (Gollancz, London 1933; new revised edition, Faber & Faber, London 1957). — Georges BLIN, *Baudelaire* (Gallimard, Paris 1939). — Jean PRÉVOST, *Baudelaire. Essai sur l'inspiration poétique* (Mercure de France, Paris 1953; reprinted 1964). — M.A. RUFF, *L'Esprit du mal et l'esthétique baudelairienne* (Armand Colin, Paris 1955). — Lloyd James AUSTIN, *L'Univers poétique de Baudelaire* (Mercure de France, Paris 1956).

b) *Particular Aspects*

Robert VIVIER, *L'Originalité de Baudelaire* (Duculot, Brussels 1926; reprinted 1962 and 1965). — Jean POMMIER, *La Mystique de Baudelaire* (Les Belles Lettres, Paris 1932; Slatkine Reprints, Geneva 1967). — André FERRAN, *L'Esthétique de Baudelaire* (Hachette, Paris 1933; new edition 1967). — Albert FEUILLERAT, *L'Architecture des "Fleurs du Mal"* (Yale University Press, New Haven 1941). — Margaret GILMAN, *Baudelaire the Critic* (Columbia University Press, New York 1943). — Jean POMMIER, *Dans les chemins de Baudelaire* (José Corti, Paris 1945). — Jean-Paul SARTRE, *Baudelaire* (Editions du Point du Jour, Paris 1946; first published as an introduction to an edition of Baudelaire's *Ecrits intimes*, this study was issued separately the following year). — Benjamin FONDANE, *Baudelaire et l'expérience du gouffre* (Seghers, Paris 1947). — Georges BLIN, *Le Sadisme de Baudelaire* (José Corti, Paris 1948). — Georges POULET, *Baudelaire*, in *Etudes sur le temps humain*, Ch. XVI (Plon, Paris 1950). — Gerhard HESS, *Die Landschaft in Baudelaires "Fleurs du Mal"* (Carl Winter, Heidelberg 1953). — J.D. HUBERT, *L'Esthétique des "Fleurs du Mal". Essai sur l'ambiguïté poétique* (Cailler, Geneva 1953). — Martin TURNELL, *Baudelaire. A Study of his Poetry* (Hamish Hamilton, London 1953). — Jean-Pierre RICHARD, *Profondeur de Baudelaire*, in *Poésie et profondeur* (Editions du Seuil, Paris 1955, pp. 93-162). — Lucie HORNER, *Baudelaire critique de Delacroix* (Droz, Geneva 1956). — Gita MAY, *Diderot et Baudelaire critiques d'art* (Droz, Geneva, and Minard, Paris 1957). — Daniel VOUGA, *Baudelaire et Joseph de Maistre* (José Corti, Paris 1957). — Pierre-Jean JOUVE, *Tombeau de Baudelaire* (Editions du Seuil, Paris 1958). — Alison FAIRLIE, *Baudelaire: "Les Fleurs du Mal"* (Edwin Arnold, London 1960; 3rd edition 1965). — Georges POULET, *Baudelaire*, in *Les métamorphoses du cercle*, Ch. XIV (Plon, Paris 1961). — Léon BOPP, *Psychologie des "Fleurs du Mal"* (Droz, Geneva 1964-1966, 3 vols.). — Charles MAURON, *Le dernier Baudelaire* (José Corti, Paris 1966). — Pierre EMMANUEL, *Baudelaire* (Les Ecrivains devant Dieu, Desclée-De Brouwer, Paris 1967). — Albert KIES, *Etudes baudelairiennes* (Nauwelaerts, Louvain and Paris 1967). — Max MILNER, *Baudelaire. Enfer ou ciel, qu'importe!* (Plon, Paris 1967). — Claude PICHOIS, *Baudelaire, Etudes et témoignages* (Editions de la Baconnière, Neuchâtel 1967).

c) *Special Issues of Magazines and Congress Proceedings*

1957-1958: *Revue d'histoire littéraire de la France* (October-December 1957). — *Revue des sciences humaines* (January-March 1957 and January-March 1958).

1967-1968: *Europe* (April-May 1967). — *Revue d'histoire littéraire de la France* (April-June 1967). — *La Table ronde* (May 1967). — *Revue des sciences humaines* (July-September 1967). — *Etudes littéraires* (Laval University, April 1968). — *Preuves* (May and December 1968).

Journées Baudelaire (Namur-Brussels, October 10-13, 1967), proceedings of the colloquy, Académie royale de langue et de littérature française, Brussels 1968. — *Baudelaire*, proceedings of the colloquy at Nice (May 25-27, 1968), Minard, Paris 1968.

Language and Style

Albert CASSAGNE, *Versification et métrique de Baudelaire* (Hachette, Paris 1906). — J.B. RATERMANIS, *Etude sur le style de Baudelaire d'après les "Fleurs du Mal" et les "Petits Poèmes en prose"* (Editions Art et Science, Baden 1949). — W.T. BANDY, *Word-Index to Baudelaire's Poems* (Madison, Wis. 1939). — Robert T. CARGO, *A Concordance to Baudelaire's "Les Fleurs du Mal"* (University of North Carolina Press, Chapel Hill 1965). — B. QUEMADA, *Baudelaire, "Les Fleurs du Mal": concordances, index et relevés statistiques* (Larousse, Paris 1965). — Pierre GUIRAUD, "Le Champ stylistique du gouffre baudelairien," *Orbis litterarum* (Copenhagen 1958, pp. 75-84). — Gérald ANTOINE, "Pour une explication 'stylistique' du gouffre baudelairien," *Le Français moderne*, April 1958, pp. 81-98. — Roman JAKOBSON and Claude LÉVI-STRAUSS, "*Les Chats* de Charles Baudelaire," *L'Homme*, January-April 1962, pp. 5-21. — Michael RIFFATERRE, "Two Approaches to Baudelaire's Les Chats," *Yale Studies*, Vol. 36-37, 1966, pp. 200-242.

The Legacy of Baudelaire

Marcel RAYMOND, *De Baudelaire au Surréalisme* (Correa, Paris 1933; new edition, José Corti, Paris 1940, reprinted several times). — Hugo FRIEDRICH, *Die Struktur der modernen Lyrik von Baudelaire bis zur Gegenwart* (Rowohlt, Hamburg 1956; new edition 1967).

LIST OF ILLUSTRATIONS

PUBLISHED AUGUST 1969

TEXT AND ILLUSTRATIONS PRINTED IN OFFSET
BY IMPRIMERIES RÉUNIES S.A., LAUSANNE
UNDER THE TECHNICAL DIRECTION OF
ÉDITIONS D'ART ALBERT SKIRA, GENEVA

PHOTOGRAPHIC CREDITS

All the photographs for this book were made by Maurice Babey, Basel, except for those obligingly placed at our disposal by the University of Virginia Library, Charlottesville, Virginia (page 73), Wadsworth Atheneum, Hartford, Connecticut (page 106), British Museum, London (pages 60 lower left, 80), National Gallery, London (pages 55 lower left, 96, 114 bottom), Middlebury College, Middlebury, Vermont (page 98 upper right), Metropolitan Museum of Art, New York (page 48), Bibliothèque Nationale, Paris (page 102 upper left and right), National Collection of Fine Arts, Smithsonian Institution, Washington, D.C. (page 54 upper left), A.C.L., Brussels (pages 45 lower right, 123, 124), Archives Photographiques, Paris (page 69 upper left), Gad Borel-Boissonnas, Geneva (pages 14, 15), J.A. Bricet, Paris (page 28), John R. Freeman, Ltd, London (page 57 lower right), and Réalités, Paris (pages 32, 116).

Printed in Switzerland